CAMBRIDGE STUDIES IN LINGUISTICS

General Editors: J. BRESNAN, B. COMRIE, W. DRESSLER,
R. LASS, D. LIGHTFOOT, J. LYONS, P.H. MATTHEWS,
R. POSNER, S. ROMAINE, N.V. SMITH, N. VINCENT

Discourse structure and anaphora

In this series

Supplementary volumes

DISCOURSE STRUCTURE AND ANAPHORA

Written and conversational English

BARBARA A. FOX

University of Colorado, Boulder

CAMBRIDGE
UNIVERSITY PRESS

Published by the Press Syndicate of the University of Cambridge
The Pitt Building, Trumpington Street, Cambridge CB2 1RP
40 West 20th Street, New York, NY 10011–4211, USA
10 Stamford Road, Oakleigh, Melbourne 3166, Australia

First published 1987
First paperback edition 1993

Printed in Great Britain at the University Press, Cambridge

British Library cataloguing in publication data

Fox, Barbara A.
Discourse structure and anaphora:
written and conversational English. –
(Cambridge studies in linguistics)
1. English language – Discourse analysis
I. Title
425   PE1422

Library of Congress cataloguing in publication data

Fox, Barbara A.
Discourse structure and anaphora.
(Cambridge studies in linguistics; 48)
Bibliography.
Includes index.
1. English language – Anaphora.
2. English language – Discourse analysis.
3. English language – Spoken English.
I. Title.   II. Series.
PE 1398.A52F6   1987   420'.141   86–33349

ISBN 0 521 33082 3 hardback
ISBN 0 521 43990 6 paperback

Contents

Preface

It is almost always a mistake to put a single author's name on a piece of research. This is especially true for the present study, since so many people have had more than a passing influence on the ideas and methods used. Most of the real work of this project was done while I was studying with Bill Mann, Manny Schegloff, and Sandy Thompson, who, in spite of their different approaches, all encouraged me, and helped create what is here now. Without their constant support, this study would never have been possible.

Sandy Chung, Jack Du Bois, Talmy Givón, Paul Hopper, and Paul Schachter have all contributed, sometimes unknowingly, to my general philosophy of language and to my appreciation of other languages. Their influence pervades the text in a somewhat less visible way, but it is still there.

My latest thinking about discourse and grammar has been shaped by colleagues at the University of Colorado, most notably Walter Kintsch and Paul Smolensky. They have increased my appreciation for what cognitive psychology and computer science have to offer linguistics, and have been instrumental in making Colorado an exciting place to be.

Many friends, colleagues, and family members have provided support for the efforts realized here. To my parents I owe the greatest debt, for always being understanding about everything. Loralee MacPike provided support and encouragement for many years, and still does, at a distance. Alan Bell, Milton Clark, Susanna Cumming, Sarah Gilbert, JoAnn Silverstein, Gina Schwartz, and Fay Wouk have at various times lent me ears to bend and shoulders to cry on. A special warm thanks to Anne Hockmeyer.

I am grateful to the National Science Foundation (NSF) for a graduate fellowship which enabled me to concentrate completely on the research for this project, and to the Institute of Cognitive Science at the University of Colorado, Boulder, for providing release time for the final writing.

The material presented here as rhetorical structure analysis is derived by my own musings from rhetorical structure theory as developed by Mann, Matthiessen, and Thompson (1982). Those authors are in no way responsible for the use I have made of their theory, or for the way in which I have presented it.

Many thanks to all.

BARBARA A. FOX
Boulder, Colorado

The royalties from the paperback edition of this book will be donated to Pūnana Leo o Honolulu, a Hawaiian language immersion preschool for the children of O'ahu.

1 *Introduction*

1.1 Major themes of the study

The last ten years have seen a tremendous upsurge in work on discourse production and comprehension, correlated with a growing concern in a variety of disciplines with language as it is used in context. Because of its fundamental place in the understanding of memory, discourse structure and semantic interpretation, anaphora has been the focus of much of this research (e.g. Grosz 1977; Reichman 1981; Sidner 1983; Tyler and Marslen-Wilson 1982; Webber 1983; Givón 1983; Halliday and Hasan 1976; Bosch 1983; Linde 1979; Reinhart 1983). Central to this work has been the belief that there is a strong relationship between the flow of information in a text, the structure of the text, and use of anaphora. A recurrent, and intuitively appealing, finding of this work is that referents which are "in focus" or "in the hearer's consciousness" can be pronominalized, where focus or consciousness are operationalized in terms of the discourse structure (see in particular Grosz 1977 and Reichman 1981).

The present study holds to this interpretation of the relationship between discourse structure and anaphora. One of the themes that runs through this study is that any treatment of anaphora must seek its understanding in the hierarchical structure of the text-type being used as a source of data. Texts may be produced and heard/read in a linear fashion, but they are designed and understood hierarchically, and this fact has dramatic consequences for the linguistic coding employed.

But, while sharing this common background with earlier works, this study departs from them in several critical ways. Because of the (natural) emphasis in cognitive science on information processing, work in the area of discourse structure has tended to view discourse as organized purely in terms of information flow and propositional content. This view is limited in two ways: it ignores the critical role played in all text-types by social, interactional, and affective factors (Linde 1979, van Dijk and Kintsch 1983, and Duranti 1984 are important exceptions); and relatedly, it fails to take into consideration the fact that texts are organized as they are not just because of informational limitations (what Dillon (1981) calls channel limitations) but also because of socially accepted conventions (cf. Wittgenstein 1958 on language games). As Dillon (1981: 15) has said:

> The general point is that if we abstract 'conveying propositional content' as the common property of written discourses, we have woefully impoverished the notion of *discourse* as a human communicative act. Or, to put it another way, we have created an enormously artificial model of discourse and have obliterated from our view the elaborate sets of conventions governing particular discourse types and the ways these can be employed to signal diverse and complex intentions.

The present study, in attempting to provide a complete account of the distribution of a subset of anaphora – reference to third-person singular humans – in conversation and expository prose, brings out the social as well as informational aspects of the relationship between discourse and anaphora. We will see that interactional and affective factors, as well as genre-specific conventions, do indeed play a significant role in anaphoric patterning in conversation and writing.

I have limited the scope of this study to third-person singular human references. I have narrowed the domain in this way to look at anaphora in its prototypical use: tracking a participant through a discourse (Du Bois 1980; what Prince (1981) would consider textually evoked references). Other uses of anaphora, such as the *this* in example (1) and *they* in example (2) below, introduce further complexities: for example, they may refer to previous utterances, rather than to participants – example (1) – or they may not refer at all (in the sense of being non-referential: Du Bois 1980) – example (2).

(1) Americans love apple pie. *This* is something to wonder at.
(2) This street has gotten very noisy recently. I think *they*'re putting up a new apartment building.

These functions of various anaphoric devices are interesting and deserve further study, but they represent complexities beyond the function of repeated references to an entity over time, and I have thus chosen not to include them in the present study.[1]

Since I am interested here in the relationships between higher-level discourse considerations and anaphora, the patterns of anaphora I have examined represent what some have called "discourse anaphora" (related to what Bosch (1983) has called *referential* pronouns), in that the instances analyzed here are not controlled syntactically (see Reinhart 1983 for a thorough discussion of syntactically controlled anaphora; Bolinger 1977 takes up similar phenomena from a functional perspective). Thus, I did not examine anaphora of the sort illustrated in the following sentences:

(3)   Zelda adores *her* teachers.
(4)   Rosa$_i$ complained that *she*$_i$ had a headache. (Reinhart, 1983)

The analyses presented in this study include the patterning of pronouns and full noun phrases in the environment of other referents (both same-gender and different-gender). I have included these patterns because such cases provide crucial information towards understanding how people manage potentially complex and "ambiguous" referring situations. In fact, to some extent it is possible to understand what counts as cognitively complex or ambiguous only by exploring such patterns.[2] I also felt that it was important to determine exactly what kind of referent (in addition to what kind of structural environment) counted as problematic, hence the division of referents into same and different gender.

The data for this study consist of (1) naturally occurring face-to-face and telephone conversations, and (2) small newspaper and magazine articles and segments of a psychoanalytic biography. Because of the theoretical orientation adopted here, which states that anaphora correlates at least in part with hierarchical discourse structure, it was necessary to "parse" these texts into their component units, so that an understanding of the relationships between anaphoric patterning and discourse structure could be achieved. For this task, I chose two different analytic tools, one for each of the two modalities: conversational analysis, developed to structurally analyze spontaneous conversation (Sacks *et al.* 1974); and rhetorical structure analysis, designed for planned expository prose (Mann *et al.* 1982; Matthiessen and Thompson forthcoming).

The use of two fairly distinct models for the two types of texts is based on the belief that the modes are fundamentally different in the units that serve to organize them. Written monologue texts are by definition produced by one person, and the units of a descriptive model should reflect this basic one-party-ness; conversational texts, on the other hand, are by definition produced by more than one person, and the units of a text model should also reflect this fact. In addition, written monologue texts are largely information-oriented, and the structural units of an appropriate model should capture the types of informational relationships that can hold between pieces of text, since these relationships give the texts their hierarchical structure (Decker 1974; Graesser and Goodman 1985);

conversational texts, on the other hand, are largely interactional, and the units of an appropriate model should capture the social action relationships that hold between pieces of talk, inasmuch as it is these more-than-one-party actions which structure the talk (see Rubin 1980 for a discussion of these and other differences between written and "spoken" language). Thus, while there are clearly interactional and affective aspects of written monologue texts and informational aspects of conversational texts, these are not the fundamental structuring units for that mode. It has therefore been critical in this work to use one model which focuses on the informational relationships between propositions for the written monologue texts and another which focuses on the interactional relationships between utterances for the conversational texts. From the small set of candidates for each type I selected conversational analysis and rhetorical structure analysis. Inasmuch as these approaches are likely to be unfamiliar to most readers, they will each be described in detail in their own chapters.

1.2   Organization

The remainder of the study is organized as follows: Chapter 2 gives an introduction to the method of structural analysis used for the conversational data, conversational analysis. The basic units of the model are discussed, and example passages are analyzed. This chapter is background for Chapter 3, which details the actual anaphoric patterns found in the conversational texts. Chapter 3 formulates the anaphoric patterns found in the conversational material. It lays out the patterns of anaphora in the conversational material in terms of the hierarchic organization of the texts. Structural patterns, as well as non-structural ones (i.e those performing other functions), are explored. Chapter 4 gives an introduction to the method of structural analysis used for the monologue expository written texts, rhetorical structure analysis. The basic units of the model are discussed, and example passages are analyzed. This chapter provides the background needed for the analyses offered in Chapter 5. Chapter 5 formulates the patterns of anaphora found in the expository written texts, using rhetorical structure analysis as the tool for exploring the structural designs of the texts. The patterns of anaphora offered in this chapter, as in previous chapters, are presented in terms of the hierarchic organization of the texts in which they occur. Chapter 6 compares the anaphoric patterning established for the conversational and expository texts using quantitative and qualitative methods of comparison. Evidence is presented which demonstrates that the two text-types differ fairly strikingly in the distribution of anaphors they display. Chapter 7 offers thoughts on the theoretical issues of localness of patterning and the nature of discourse structure.

2 Conversational analysis

This chapter is meant as an overview of the fundamental concepts of conversational analysis which will be put to work in Chapter 3. It is by no means a complete guide to this approach; I have included only those notions which will be applied in the analyses in Chapter 3. For a more complete introduction to CA, see Levinson 1983 or Atkinson and Drew 1979. Readers already familiar with CA can skip to Chapter 3.[1]

2.1 Notation conventions

Before we examine some of the substantive findings of conversational analysis, I would like to present and discuss some of the notational conventions used in CA-style transcripts. Many of these conventions may be unfamiliar to linguists, but they are all in fact fairly straightforward. (The sources of the transcripts reproduced in this book are given in abbreviated form – AD:14, SN-4:30, etc. – at the end of the extracts. Further details of these sources are given in section 3.2.)

All talk is transcribed in a pseudo-phonetic system, using the basic orthographic symbols of written English; that is, if the speaker pronounces a word in a way that is not the only possible pronunciation for that word, then special care is taken to transcribe that particular pronunciation (but without using a special alphabet). This practice makes the transcripts somewhat difficult to read (especially for the non-native speaker), but since it brings out useful information I have not normalized the transcripts (except for crucial pronouns, which have been normalized for ease of reading and exposition).

The double slash (//) indicates the place at which a speaker's utterance is overlapped by talk from another speaker.

> M. No. They're a//ll thin.]
> C. They're not]

(AD:14)

Thus with this notation we can see that C's utterance starts after the *a* in M's *all*. The right-hand bracket (]) indicates the place in the utterance at which the overlap ends (so C's overlap lasts until after M's *thin*).

An utterance which has more than one double slash in it is overlapped at more than one place, and the utterances which do the overlapping are given in sequential order after the overlapped utterance.

> G. they're all Keegans like the ones around <u>Green</u>springs
>   they're all kind'v, // bout five five, five si//x,
> M. They're all <u>from</u> around Greensprin//gs.
> C. Yeh

$$(AD:14)$$

Here, M's utterance overlaps G's starting at *bout*, and C's utterance overlaps G's starting with the *x* in *six*. Notice that C's utterance also overlaps the very end of M's.

A left-hand bracket at the beginning of two lines indicates that the two utterances begin simultaneously.

> M. Yeh.
>   [
> C. Lo:ng time ago it reminds me

$$(AD:14)$$

The equals sign (=) indicates latching, that is, the next speaker begins without the usual "beat" of silence after the current speaker finishes talking. In this case there is an equals sign at the end of the current speaker's utterance and another equals sign at the beginning of the next speaker's utterance. If two speakers simultaneously latch onto a preceding utterance (that is, they begin talking simultaneously), this is indicated in the transcript with a left-hand bracket preceded by an equals sign.

> (R) (h)hh (h)uh (h)uh (h)uh!=
> (S) hhh(h) H(h)m]
>   =[
> K. Which la:]mpost?

$$(SN-4:30)$$

Here S and K simultaneously latch onto R's laughter.

Numbers given in parentheses indicate elapsed silence, measured in tenths of seconds. Single parentheses with a raised dot between them represent a silence that is less than a tenth of a second but still longer than the usual beat of silence. These figures are not arrived at with a stop-watch, but are calculated with a verbal counting technique which takes into account the tempo of the preceding talk. Thus a silence which is timed at 0.3 of a second in one stretch of talk might well be timed at something else in another stretch of talk if the tempo of the preceding talk is different. The numbers thus indicate "experiential time" rather than chronological time.

Certain facts about the production of the talk are given through the orthographic symbols used. Punctuation is used to suggest intonation; underlining indicates stress. A colon after a letter means that the sound represented by that letter is somewhat lengthened; a series of colons means that the sound is increasingly lengthened. Anything preceded by a degree mark is quiet.

The letter *h* within parentheses indicates "explosive aspiration," and usually means some type of laughter is being produced. A series of *h*s preceded by a raised dot represents an inbreath (where number of *h*s is meant to correspond to the length of inbreath), while the same series preceded by nothing represents exhaling. Capitalization is used to indicate increased volume.

Questionable transcriptions are enclosed within single parentheses; the transcribers thereby indicate that the exact form of the utterance is not clear. Speaker's initials given in single parentheses means that there is some question about the speaker's identity. Double parentheses – e.g. ((clears throat)) – represent non-transcribed material (i.e., noise which is non-linguistic).

These are the major transcription conventions which will be used in the data fragments in this and later chapters. For a more detailed guide to CA notational conventions, see Sacks *et al.* 1974.[2]

To help the reader identify the structure of some of the passages, I have created a simple system of labeling which indicates which adjacency pair an utterance belongs to, what level of structure it is to be heard at, and whether it is a first-pair part, a second-pair part, or a third-position utterance. This simple system works in the following way.

The label has three slots: the first indicates the position in the adjacency pair – first-pair part, etc. – that the utterance fills (first-pair part is abbreviated *fpp*, second-pair part *spp*). So, for example, the following invented example has two utterances, the first labeled *fpp*, the second *spp*.

> A.   Do you have a computer at home?   [fpp]
> B.   No.   [spp]

The second slot in the label reflects a sequential numbering of the adjacency pairs. The first adjacency in a cited passage is given the number 1, the second adjacency pair the number 2, and so on. The numbering is done strictly by temporal ordering. All parts of a single adjacency pair (i.e. the first-pair part and the second-pair part, along with any third-position utterance) are given the same number. In the following example, we have two adjacency pairs:

B.	hh Hey do you see v- (0.3) fat ol' Vivian anymouh?	[fpp (1)]
A.	No, hardly, en if we do:, y'know, I just say hello quick'n ·hh y'know, jus' pass each othuh in th//e hall.	[spp (1)]
B.	Is she still hangin aroun (with) Bo:nny?	[fpp (2)]
		(TG:14)

Notice that the fpp and the spp of the first pair are both assigned the number 1, while the fpp of the next pair is assigned the number 2.

The third slot of the label indicates the level of structure at which the utterance fits in (members of a single adjacency pair are treated as being at the same level of structure). For example, if we have an announcement pair followed by a post-elaboration question–answer pair, the announcement pair will be labeled as being at a higher level of structure than the post-elaboration (lower-case letters are used for this slot, beginning with *a*). This labeling is meant to capture the impression that the announcement in such a situation is somehow nuclear, or core, and the post-elaboration is somehow embedded, or subordinate, or adjunct. An example of this labeling follows:

M.	A:nd ( ) as far as that goes my father's on his honeymoon. =	[fpp (1,a)]
	=(y:ah ha ha°ha)	
K.	(Oh::.) Very nice=	[spp (1,a)]
K.	=Where'd he go.	[fpp (2,b)]
		(SN-4:10)

M's utterance is a first-pair part (fpp), and is in the first adjacency pair of the fragment (1). In addition, it is at the highest level of structure of the fragment (a). K's first utterance possesses all of the same features, except that it is a second-pair part (spp). K's second utterance, on the other hand, is different: it is the beginning of the second adjacency pair, and it is at an "embedded" level of structure with regard to the first pair (indicated by the letter *b*).

This notation system is meant to provide a "map" for some of the fragments presented in Chapter 3. It has no theoretical status, and is offered only as a simple schematic guide for the reader.

2.2   The turn-taking system

One of the most critical aspects of conversational structure is turn-taking. How are turns allocated in informal conversation? To answer this question we need to establish some rudimentary facts about turns.

We need to first establish that there are units out of which turns can be constructed. These units have been referred to as *turn-constructional units* (TCUs), and can be single lexical items (*yes*, for example), phrases, clauses, or sentences. According to the turn-taking system, each speaker is at first allotted one of these TCUs. The end of such a unit constitutes a place where speaker-change could occur: that is, at this point another person could begin talking. The end of a TCU is thus a *transition-relevance place* (TRP), since it is a place at which a transition from one speaker to another can (but need not) occur.

The following turn-taking rules, which are based on these concepts, are taken verbatim from Levinson (1983, which is based on Sacks *et al.* 1974):

Rule 1 – applies initially at the first TRP of any turn:

(a) If the current speaker selects a next speaker in current turn, then current speaker must stop speaking, and that next speaker must speak next, transition occurring at the first TRP after next-speaker selection.

(b) If current speaker does not select next speaker, then any (other) party may self-select, first speaker gaining rights to the next turn.

(c) If current speaker does not select next speaker, and no other party self-selects under option (b), then current speaker may (but need not) continue.

Rule 2 – applies at all subsequent TRPs:
  When rule 1(c) has been applied by the current speaker, then at the next TRP rules 1(a)–(c) apply, and recursively at the next TRP, until speaker change is effected.

These rules provide a foundation for making sense out of two related phenomena: simultaneous talk and silence.

Simultaneous talk obviously occurs when two (or more) speakers talk at once. But not all simultaneous talk represents a violation of the turn-taking system rules. Rather, there are two basic types of simultaneous talk (i.e. overlap): competitive overlap and non-competitive overlap. In one type of non-competitive overlap, called terminal overlap, the current speaker approaches the end of a turn-constructional unit and, as that is happening, the next speaker, having predicted the type of TCU that the current speaker is producing, starts talking, thus overlapping with the very end of the TCU which the current speaker was heard to be constructing. This type of overlap is not heard as competitive. In addition, laughter from one party simultaneous with talk from another party is often not heard as competitive (but appreciative). An example of terminal (non-competitive) overlap is given below.

    N.   Also he sid that (0.3) ·t what you ea:t, (0.2) end how you
          wash yer face has _nothing tih do with it,
              (0.8)
    H.   Yer _kiddin//g.
    N.   nNo:_,

                                            (HG:II:4–5)

In competitive overlap, on the other hand, the rules of the turn-taking system are violated, usually by the next speaker starting up before the projected transition relevance place of the current speaker's TCU. An example of competitive overlap follows.

    H.   En I nearly wen'chh_razy cz I//: l:_lo:ve that mo:vie.
    N.   y:_Yeah I _know you lo:ve tha::t.

                                            (HG:II:8)

In this passage H is not near the end of a TCU (she has just produced the subject of a subordinate clause) when N starts up.

Competitively overlapping utterances can be characterized by higher pitch, slower tempo, louder volume, and lengthened vowels.

Silence occurs, obviously, when no one is talking. Not all silences are equivalent, however. Silence is considered a *pause* if it is attributable, by the turn-taking system, to a given party; for example, if current speaker has selected next speaker, then any silence after current speaker reaches the end of his/her TCU is a pause attributable to the selected next speaker. The following is an example of two pauses, both attributable to speaker B (example taken from Levinson 1983, which I follow in this definition of gaps and pauses, the latter of which Levinson calls "attributable silences"):

    A.   Is there something bothering you or not?
             (1.0)
    A.   Yes or no
             (1.5)
    A.   Eh?
    B.   No.

Silence is considered a *gap*, on the other hand, if it is not attributable, by the turn-taking system, to any particular party. This situation often arises if the current speaker has not selected a next speaker, and the silence therefore "belongs" to no one (although the current speaker can apply rule 1(c) and get another turn at talk, and in certain cases this will create the effect that the preceding silence was in fact attributable to the current speaker). An example of a gap is given below.

```
N.   = ˙hhh Dz he av his own apa:rt//mint?
H.   ˙hhhh Yea:h, =
N.   =Oh:,
              (1.0)
N.   How didju git his number
```
                                                                    (HG:II:25)

The turn-taking system proposed by Sacks *et al.* (1974) affords insight into many other aspects of conversation, but for our purposes here the concepts covered above will suffice.

2.3   The structural organization of conversation

The next facet of conversational analysis which will be crucial for the analyses presented in Chapter 3 is the identification of the structural organization of conversation, through the basic unit of the adjacency pair.

An adjacency pair is said to consist of two parts, the first of which (the first-pair part) makes relevant a particular type of action (the second-pair part) from another party. In fact, it is not altogether clear that there should only be two parts in a "pair", nor is it clear that the parts need to be adjacent. These problems with the literal interpretation of the term "adjacency pair" need not concern us here.

We thus have first actions which make relevant second actions by another party. Standard examples of the notion of adjacency pair are question–answer, invitation–acceptance, offer–acceptance, request–comply, and announcement–assessment.

An adjacency pair, or sequence, can take three types of expansions: pre-expansions, insert expansions, and post-expansions (see Levinson 1983 for a discussion). A pre-expansion is an adjacency pair that comes before another adjacency pair and is preliminary to it. A classic example of a pre-expansion is the pre-announcement adjacency pair, which usually consists of a pre-announcement first-pair part and a clearance second-pair part:

A. Guess what?
B. What?
A. I got an IBM PC!
B. That's great!

(Invented example)

An insert expansion is an adjacency pair which comes between the first-pair part and the second-pair part of another adjacency pair. Question–answer pairs are common insert expansions:

A. May I speak to President Reagan?
B. May I ask who's calling?
A. Nancy.
B. Ok.

(Invented example)

Notice that the insert expansion pair is completed before the other pair continues.

A post-expansion is a pair which follows another pair. If, for example, an adjacency pair that seeks to repair some source of trouble in a preceding turn (known as a repair sequence) is initiated after the possible completion of an adjacency pair, the repair sequence will be considered a post-expansion:

A. Do you like Virginia?
B. Yeah.
A. You do?
B. Well, not really.

(Invented example)

It is worth taking a brief excursion at this point into the nature of repair sequences. A repair sequence is often initiated with what is called a "next-turn repair initiator" (NTRI), which indicates that in the next turn the next speaker ought to attend to some problem which the current speaker has encountered with the preceding turn; hence it initiates repair action for the next turn. A next-turn repair initiator does not, however, only indicate technical difficulties with hearing, etc.: it often indicates that the speaker of the NTRI is about to disagree with the preceding turn (as in the invented example above). A frequent response to this pre-disagreement in the surface guise of an NTRI is a backdown, in which the next speaker backs down from the utterance which triggered the disagreement (as in the example above).

For the purposes of this study, I have identified two other pair relations and one turn relation: member of a series, post-elaboration, and turn expansion. These relations should be taken as tentative; they have not been subjected to the rigorous testing against large numbers of corpora which characterizes the relations described above.

In a series, one adjacency pair is "tied" to another pair by virtue of being another in a member of the same series, that is, by being a "next" in a series of similar items. We can find a series of topic proffers, or a series of requests, etc. An example of the series relation is given below.

> B.   ·hh Hey do you see v- (0.3) fat ol' Vivian
> anymouh?
> A.   No, hardly, en if we do:, y'know, I just say
> hello quick'n ·hh y'know, jus' pass each othuh
> in th//e hall.
> B.   Is she still hangin aroun (with) Bo:nny?
>
> (TG:14)

B's second turn in this passage is a second in a series of topic proffers.

In a post-elaboration, one pair gives a piece of news, or makes a report, and a subsequent pair gives or seeks details about that piece of news or report. An example of this relation follows.

> M.   A:nd   (   ) as far as that goes my father's on his
> honeymoon. =
> = (y:ah ha ha°ha)
> K.   (Oh::.) Very nice=
> K.   =Where'd he go.
>
> (SN-4:10)

K's second line is a post-elaboration on the preceding adjacency pair, since it seeks details about the general piece of news given in M's utterance.

In a turn expansion, a single turn – which had come to a possible completion place – is continued by the speaker self-selecting (following rule 1(c) of the turn-taking system). An example of this relation follows.

> G.   I usetuh go over there wih my cousin (over that track),
> (1.2)
> G.   His name wz uh, Tucker.
>
> (AD:17)

G's second line in this passage is a turn expansion.

2.4   Conclusion

These are the major conventions and concepts that will enter our discussion of anaphora in conversation in Chapter 3. Additional material about this method of analysis can be found in Levinson 1983; Atkinson and Drew 1979; Schegloff and Sacks 1973; Goodwin 1981; Terasaki 1976; Pomerantz 1975; Schegloff *et al.* 1977; and Schenkein 1978. Material about a related method of analysis can be found in Burton 1980 and Coulthard and Montgomery 1981.

3 Anaphora in conversational English

3.1 Introduction

In this chapter, I discuss the distribution of pronouns and full noun phrases in non-story conversational texts.

In presenting the distributions, I operate in two modes of description, one of which can be thought of as the "context-determines-use" mode, the other the "use-accomplishes-context" mode. In the context-determines-use mode, it is assumed that the hierarchic structure of the talk *determines* to some large extent the anaphoric form which the speaker is to use. The type of pattern offered in this mode says that in context X the speaker will use anaphoric form Y. In the use-accomplishes-context mode, on the other hand, it is assumed that it is by virtue of using a particular anaphoric form that the structure is created.

I have assumed in this study that both modes of operation are always present for the participants. That is, for the most part knowledge about how anaphora is usually handled in certain contexts leads a participant to pick the anaphoric form that is "unmarked" for the context, and by picking this form the participant displays his/her understanding of what type of context is currently under development: this display of understanding, in turn, can create for the other parties present the same understanding (when by themselves they might have constructed some other sort of understanding of the current structure). There is thus a continuous interaction, even in the simplest cases, of the following three steps of reasoning:

1 Anaphoric form X is the "unmarked" form for a context like the one the participant is in now.
2 By using anaphoric form X, then, the participant displays a belief that the context is of a particular sort.
3 If the participant displays a belief that the context is of a particular sort, then the other parties may change their beliefs about the nature of the context to be in accord with the belief displayed.

In this way, an anaphoric choice at once is determined by and itself determines the structure of the talk. It should thus be kept in mind that while some statements of distribution sound as though they belong in one mode rather than another, all of the patterns are meant to accommodate the interaction of both modes.

One further note about the assumptions of this chapter is in order here. I have assumed that the basic pattern of anaphora (presented below) and the patterns for different-gender and same-gender environments represent the unmarked uses of anaphora, in which the speaker can be heard to be doing "nothing special" except displaying an understanding of the current structure of the talk. The patterns described under the heading of non-structural factors, on the other hand, are offered as the "marked" uses of anaphora, with which the speaker is heard to be doing something special interactionally (such as disagreeing). In this view, anaphora is not determined just by referent-tracking, structuring considerations; it is also *manipulated* to accomplish certain interactional tasks.

3.2 The data

The conversational data examined in this study cover a fairly broad range. Telephone and face-to-face, two parties and several parties, single gender and mixed gender, video-tape and audio-tape, are all represented in the pool. The conversations were chosen randomly within a set of fixed criteria: they had to be spontaneous, naturally occurring conversations (rather than produced in an experimental or induced setting) between friends or relatives, and they had to contain at least one segment in which at least one person was referred to more than once. They also had to be transcribed within the tradition of conversational analysis (see Sacks *et al.* 1974 and Chapter 2 of this study for a discussion of transcription practices within this framework). In addition, the passages had to be non-narrative in nature (see the discussion below on the comparability of discourse-types, in which I suggest that expository written texts are in some sense comparable to non-narrative conversational passages), where narratives are considered to be relatings of a series of sequenced events. The names of each transcript, and a brief description of the interactants involved, are given below (very little ethnographic information is available for these interactions).[1]

1   *TG*. A telephone interaction between two college-aged women friends. Audio-tape.
2   *SN-4*. A face-to-face, multi-party interaction, involving three college-aged

women and one college-aged man (with a brief appearance of another same-aged woman), all of whom appear to know the others.   Audio-tape.

3   *AD.*   A face-to-face, multi-party (outdoors) interaction involving three coup-les, most of which consists of the three men talking about cars and car races.   Video-tape.

4   *Friedell.*   A face-to-face interaction between a college-aged man and woman (possibly husband and wife).   Audio-tape.

5   *HG:II.*   A telephone interaction betwen two young women friends.   Audio-tape.

6   *MTRAC:60-1:2.*   A telephone interaction between a man and a woman (formerly married to one another, now separated or divorced).   Audio-tape.

7   *US.*   A face-to-face, multi-party interaction involving as many as seven people (six men and one woman), in an upholstery shop owned by one of the participants.   Audio-tape.

8   *Clacia.*   A face-to-face interaction between two women friends.   Video-tape.

These eight transcripts form the pool of conversational data used in the study.

3.3   The basic pattern of anaphora

The basic, most unconstrained description of the distribution of anaphoric devices in non-story talk can be given as follows:

The first mention of a referent in a sequence is done with a full NP. After that, by using a pronoun the speaker displays an understanding that the preceding sequence has not been closed down.

This formulation of the distribution implies that interactants monitor the talk they are engaged in for signs of closure, and reflect to their interlocutors the result of this monitoring, at least in part, by the type of anaphoric device they choose.

Notice, too, that this pattern is framed in terms of discourse units, rather than distance or importance. This formulation runs counter to the traditional theory of anaphora (for example Givón 1983), which holds that the anaphoric device chosen by a speaker/writer is correlated with distance to the last mention of the relevant referent. We will see throughout this chapter, however, that the traditional theory of anaphora fails to account for a critical portion of the data.[2]

The basic pattern contains three subcomponents, each of which will be examined in detail below. They are:

1   The first mention of a referent in a sequence is done with a full NP.

2   After the first mention of a referent, a pronoun is used to display an understanding of the sequence as not yet closed.

3 A full NP is used to display an understanding of the preceding sequence containing other mentions of the same referent as closed.

Each of these subpatterns is taken up in the following sections.

3.3.1 Full noun phrase for first mention

The fairly obvious intuition that the first mention of a referent in a sequence is done with a full NP is supported by the following data fragments.

> B. Eh-yih have anybuddy: thet uh:?
> >   (1.2)
> B. -I would know from the English depar'mint there?
> A. Mm-mh. Tch! I don't think so.
> B. °Oh, =
> ➤ B. = Did they geh ridda Kuhleznik yet hhh
> A. No in fact I know somebuddy who has her now.

> > > > > > > (TG:6)

The first mention of Kuhleznik in the conversation is done with a full NP.

> S. She wasn't invited d'the] wedding?
> >   [
> M. (I'm g'nuh take her out.)]
> >   (1.0)
> M. (She d//oesn' wanna g]o.)
> S. (Hardly.])
> M. (   )
> M. N//o no.]
> (R). hhih] hmh-hmh
> >   (0.1)
> M. Sh's tryin t'stay away from the wedding °(idea).
> >   (1.0)
> ➤ M. A:nd ( ) (as) far as that goes my father's on his honeymoon. =

> > > > > > > (SN-4:10)

Here again the first mention of a person, M's father, is done with a full NP. One additional instance follows:

> M. Hello:?
> T. Hi: Marsha?
> M. Ye:ah.
> T. How are you.
> ➤ M. Fi::ne. Did Joey get home yet?

> > > > > > (MDE:MTRAC:60-1:2:1)

In this passage the first reference in the phone conversation to M and T's son is done with a full NP.

Although, as we will see in a later section the first mention of a referent *can* be done with a pronoun, the basic pattern is to have this mention done with a full NP.

3.3.2   Pronouns used to display that a sequence is not closed

The range of structural contexts in which speakers are likely to display a "non-closed" understanding is fairly broad; these contexts are described below.[3]

The first and most obvious instance in which a sequence is not closed is in the middle of an adjacency pair, that is, after the first-pair part of an adjacency pair. Speakers thus regularly use a pronoun in the second-pair part of an adjacency pair if the referent is mentioned in the first-pair part. Examples of this extremely common phenomenon are given below.

Question–Answer:

> H.   Dz Petersin have a copy'v the paper.th't you c'd
>   read.
> > (1.2)
> → S.   Evidently Wa:rd's not letting him, (0.6) talk about what
>   he wannid t'talk about,
> > > (Friedell:16)

> A.   Oh my mother wannduh know how's yer grandmother.
> → B.   ·hhh Uh::, (0.3) I don'know I guess she's aw-she's
>   awright
> > > (TG:3–4)

> B.   =Did they geh ridda Kuhleznik yet hhh
> → A.   No in fact I know somebuddy who has her now.
> > > (TG:6)

> M.   So (yer da:ting) Keith?
> > (1.0)
> → K.   (He's a friend.)
> > > (SN-4:29)

In each of these cases, a pronoun is used in the second-pair part of an adjacency pair when the referent is mentioned in the first-pair part of the pair. By using a pronoun in this situation, speakers display their understanding that the same sequence is in progress.

Another situation in which a sequence is not yet closed is the *turn expansion* (Schegloff, class lecture). In a turn expansion, a single turn – which had come to a possible completion place – is continued by the speaker self-selecting (following rule 1(c) of the turn-taking system). Here again we have the pattern of possible completion followed by continuation, where the continuation is effected by a pronoun. Examples of this pattern follow.[4]

> G.   I usetuh go over there wih my cousin (over that track),
>   (1.2)
> ⟶ G.   His name wz uh, Tucker.

>   (AD:17)

Here a pronoun (*his name*) is used for the continuing turn expansion. Another example follows.

> G.   I usetuh go over there the://n 'n, no:w, Rich Hawkins
>   from Bellview drives one, fer some guys frm up't Bellview.
> M.   ((clears throat))
>   (0.4)
> M.   Yah.
> ⟶ G.   He's my:: liddle sister's brother'n law.
>   (0.5)
> ⟶ G.   He's a policem'n in Bellview

>   (AD:18)

In each of the turn expansions in this passage a pronoun is used. Further examples:

> V.   When he gave me the ten my wife wz standin right deyuh 'n,
>   what'm I gonna tell (   ).
>   (1.3)
> ⟶ V.   She wantstuh get intuh my business.

>   (US:15)

> M.   and then I've got s'mething planned on Sunday with Laura,
>   (0.4)
> ⟶ M.   She she wa- she 'n I 're gonna go out en get drunk at four
>   o'clock in the afternoon

>   (SN-4:9)

The second-pair part of an adjacency pair does not necessarily signal the end of a sequence, however. A second adjacency pair can be "tied" to the first in such a way that the sequence is heard as being continued rather than closed. Pronouns, as one show of continuing something already started, are used in these cases. A clear example of this use of pronouns can be seen in

the following passage, in which an announcement first-pair part is followed
by its assessment second-pair part, which is in turn followed by the first-pair
part of a new adjacency pair: and this last utterance contains a pronoun
which refers to the person mentioned in the preceding pair.

<pre>
M.   A:nd ( ) as far as that goes my father's on his
     honeymoon. =   [fpp (1,a)]
     =(y:ah ha ha°ha)
K.   (Oh::.)   Very//nice=   [spp (1,a)]
→ K.   = Where'd he go.   [fpp (2,b)]
                                                           (SN-4:10)
</pre>

The pronoun is used in this case because the adjacency pair is possibly
complete after its second-pair part has been produced, but it is not definitely
closed. The pronoun in the second adjacency pair displays to the recipient
that the speaker heard the unit as possibly complete but has extended it.

The ways in which an adjacency pair can be "tied" (Sacks 1971) to a
preceding pair seem to be fairly limited.[5] The first type of tying is called a
series. In a series, one adjacency pair is meant to be of the same type as some
preceding pair, that is, the next in a series of similar items. The series could
be of any action-type; in other words, we can find instances of a series of
topic proffers, or of solutions to a problem, or of relevant questions about
something. It is clear that, if an item is possibly a member of series, then its
appearance should not close the adjacency pair to which it is tied (when the
last in the series is complete, the tied-to pair is possibly complete); hence a
pronoun can be used in a next member of a series. In the following passages,
for example, pronouns are used in the second member of a series (their
referents appear in the first member).[6]

Examples illustrating the use of pronoun in the second member in a series
are given below.

<pre>
B.   ·hh Hey do you see v- (0.3) fat ol' Vivian
     anymouh?   [fpp (1,a)]
A.   No, hardly, en if we do:, y'know, I jus' say hello
     quick'n,   [spp (1,a)]
     ·hh y'know, jus' pass each othuh in the hall.
→ B.   Is she still hangin aroun (with) Bo:nny?   [fpp (2,a)]
                                                           (TG:14)
</pre>

```
    M.   So (yer da:ting) Keith?                          [fpp (1,a)]
              (1.0)
    K.   (He's a friend.)                                 [spp (1,a)]
              (0.5)
→   M.   What about that girl he use tuh go with fer
         so long                                          [fpp (2,a)]
```

                                                          (SN-4:29)

In each of these cases, the first-pair part of the initial adjacency pair is a topic
proffer which is met in the second-pair part with a response. The first-pair
part of the second adjacency pair is a second topic proffer, which represents
a second attempt to get the matter talked about. In this way the second
first-pair part is another in a series started by the preceding first-pair part.

A second way in which an adjacency pair can be tied to a preceding pair is
by a relation I will call *post-elaboration*. In this relation, one pair gives a
piece of news, or makes a report, and a subsequent pair gives or seeks
(depending on who does the post-elaboration) details about that piece of
news or report (compare this relation with the elaboration relation in
rhetorical structure analysis). Once again, the initial pair can possibly be
complete when its second-pair part is produced, but a post-elaboration
continues it, and this continuing of a not definitely closed unit is displayed
by the use of a pronoun.

```
    M.   A:nd ( ) as far as that goes my father's on his
         honeymoon.=                                      [fpp (1,a)]
         =(y:ah ha ha°ha)
    K.   (Oh::.)  Very//nice=                             [spp (1,a)]
→   K.   = Where'd he go.                                 [fpp (2,b)]
```

                                                          (SN-4:10)

```
1. B.   Oh Sibbie's sistuh hadda ba:by bo:way.           [fpp (1,a)]
2. A.   Who?                                              [fpp (2,b)]
3. B.   Sibbie's sister.                                  [spp (2,b)]
4. A.   Oh really?                                        [fpp (3,b)]
5. B.   Myeah,                                            [spp (3,b)]
6. A.   °(That's nice.)                                   [spp (1,a)]
          [
→ 7. B.   She had it yestihday. Ten:: pou:nds.           [fpp (4,b)]
  8. A.   °Je:sus Christ.                                 [spp (4,b)]
```

                                                          (TG:27)

In this passage, an announcement is made at line 1, and this eventually gets its second-pair part at line 6. The sequence is at line 6, then, possibly complete, but B continues it at line 7 with a post-elaboration first-pair part, in which she gives details about the news announced at line 1. The speaker's understanding that the announcement sequence was only *possibly* complete allows her use of a pronoun at line 7, in which she continues the sequence. Another example of post-elaboration and pronominalization is given below.

    H.   And there wz a ledder fr'm Da:ve.
                   (0.4)
    S.   Dave,
    H.   My brother Da:ve.
    S.   Oh. Okay.   When you said Dayuv I went.   First
          Dave I think of is, (·) Dave Cantrun Dave Chu:n
                   (0.4)
    S.   En the(h)en,
                   (0.3)
    H.   Then David Wiser 'n // then David Jones (°I// know)
    S.   nhh!
    S.   Yea:h.
    S.   Well yer b-
                   (0.4)
    S.   He's not say//leeyent.
    H.   He i:s Da:ve//°yihknow.
    S.   he- he's not sa(h)l(h)ie(h)nt.
                   (0.6)
    H.   °°E:sh.
                   (0.9)
──▶ S.   What'd he haftuh say,

                                              (Friedell:8–9)

In this case, the post-elaboration (the last line) is produced by the recipient of the announcement, rather than by its speaker. Nonetheless, the post-elaboration is done with a pronoun, which is an indication from S that she has heard the announcement sequence as not definitely closed (in spite of the material intervening and the fact that she hasn't produced a second-pair part for the announcement).[7]

   This is an appropriate time to point out that the mention of the referent in the initial adjacency pair does not have to come in the first-pair part of that pair; it can come in the second-pair part and still be pronominalized in the post-elaboration pair. An instance of this phenomenon is given below.

```
C.  (Oh-) how wz the races las'night.
            (0.8)
().  (ha-//uh)] =
C.  Who w'n //th' feature.]
M.   = Al won,]
            (0.3)
C.  (Who)
    [        ] =
M.  Al.
C.   = Al did?
```
→ C. Dz he go out there pretty regular?

(AD:7)

In this passage, the relevant referent (A1) appears in the second-pair part of
the initial adjacency pair and yet can still be pronominalized in the first-pair
part of the post-elaboration pair begun by C in the last line. It is far more
common, however, for the mention in the initial pair to come in the
first-pair part.[8]

It is also possible, in the case of post-elaboration and the other tying
relation discussed here, that the pronoun in the tying pair will come in the
second-pair part, rather than in the first. That is, it is possible to find cases
in which a referent is mentioned in an adjacency pair and then
pronominalized in the second-pair part of the tying pair. An example of this
situation is given below.

```
 1. H.   = hhh Oh yih know w'n I wz talking
 2.        tuh Gra:ce.
 3.              (0.2)
 4. N.   °Gra//:ce,
 5. H.   Member Gra:ce?   my fren Gra//:ce,
 6. N.   Ye::ah. =
 7. H.   = hhh Ay:::u::n, ·hhhh she has, these best
 8.        frien's. =
 9. N.   = Uh hu:h,
10.            (·)
11. H.   tha:t live in: Minneapolis. 'n they have a
12.        so:n. =
13. N.   Oh:.
         = [
14. H.   who's twunny:: four'r twunny fi//ve. Sumpn,
15. N.   Uh hu:h,
16. H.   = pt·thhhh 'n he's in gra:d school i:n uhhh (·)
17.        bio chem °'r °something like tha:t, =
18. N.   = Sounds good, =
```

```
19. H.   =A:n'hhhhhh   hnh-hnh //sounds kosher? ·ihhhh=
20. N.   °(shhounds ghhhood)
21. H.   A:n' he's coming ou:t.here,
22.          (0.3)
23. H.   January twunny seventh er // something.
24.       ·t·hhh
25. N.   Mmmm::::::  :::::.
26. H.   =So: en she awready wrote him about
27.       me en evrythi//ing en she'd li:ke
28. N.   A w r i : : g h t.
29. H.   =(t') f//ix us u:p.
30. N.   Does he wanna meet you?
31.(H).  (°So),
32.               (·)
33. N.   I mean d//z he wanna-
34. H.   Well he doesn' have too much've a
35.       choi(h)oice=
36. N.   =Oh yeh that's truhh!=
37. H.   =·i- ·u- ·e:hhh,
38.          ( · )
39. H.   ·u- ·uhhhh
      [
40. N.   ·uhnuhhhh
41.          (0.2)
42. N.   Well wt's (·) wt's he li://ke.
➡ 43. H.  ·hhhhhhhh a- ah: she says
```

(HG:II:19–21)

Here, we get an announcement (H's lines 26–9) and then a series of two post-elaborations initiated by N at lines 30 and 42 (*does he want to meet you?* and *well what's he like*). The pronoun referring to Grace in the second post-elaboration (at line 43) comes not in the first-pair part, but in the second-pair part. It is clear from this sort of example – in which eleven lines separate the last mention of Grace from the most recent mention of her – that mere distance between mentions by itself is not what determines anaphoric patterns; rather, it is the structural properties of the talk that exert this influence.

Two adjacency pairs do not have to be physically contiguous for one to be tied to, as a "continuation" of, the other; they can be separated by adjacency pairs bearing one of the relations described above to the initial pair, and to one another, as long as the second of the pairs in question *returns* to the first of the pairs, that is, bears one of the above relations (i.e. series, post-elaboration, or post-expansion) directly to that pair rather than to one of the intervening pairs. In essence what I am referring to here is a situation in which a pair "ties" to a pair other than the immediately preceding one. I will call this structure a *return pop*.[9] Let me illustrate the concept of return pop, and the types of anaphoric patterning associated with it, by looking at a few examples.

```
 1. C.  He:y.   Where c'n I get a::, uh, 'member the old twenny
 2.        three Model T spring,
 3.              (0.5)
 4. C.  Backspring 't came up like that,
 5. C.  Dju know what I'm// talk] what I'm talkin a//bout,]
 6. M.  Ye:h,]
 7. M.  I thi]nk- I know whatchu mean,
 8. C.  Wh'r c'n I get o:ne.
 9.              (1.2)
10. G.  Just use a regular one.
11.              (0.7)
12. C.  Mmm I'd like t'get a, high one if I cou:ld.
13.              (0.7)
14. G.  I know uh-]
          [
15. M.   Lemme ask] a guy at work. He's gotta bunch a'
16.        old clu//nkers.
17. G.  Y'know Marlon Liddle?
18.              (0.2)
19. M.  Well I can't say they're ol' clunkers he's
20.        gotta Co:rd?
21.              (0.1)
22. M.  Two Co:rds,
23.              (1.0)
24. M.  And
          [
25. C.  Not original,
26. M.  Oh yes.  Very origi(h)nal
27. C.  Oh::: reall//y?
28. M.  Yah.  Ve(h)ry origi(h)nal.
29. C.  °Awhhh are you shittin m//e?
30. M.  No I'm not.
31.              (0.8)
→ 32. C.  What's his name.
```

(AD:22)

In this example, C produces a request for information at line 8, which M responds to with an offer (*let me ask a guy at work*). M then makes use of this offer to do something of a sly announcement (lines 19–22), in the form of a self-repair. The relevant person is mentioned in this offer/announcement. Announcement sequences often contain within them insert appreciation pairs, and in this passage, C initiates a series of three appreciation inserts (lines 25–30). Each of the three appreciation pairs is at the same level of structure as the others, and each is also "tied" to the announcement by the insert-expansion relation. None of them contains mentions of the person referred to in M's pseudo-announcement. Nonetheless, after these insert expansions, C can do a post-elaboration on the announcement, that is, do a return pop, using a pronoun to refer to the person last mentioned in the announcement. In this case, we have a nice instance of long-distance pronominalization sanctioned by the structure of the sequence.[10] A schematic representation of the passage may clarify the return pop pronominalization:

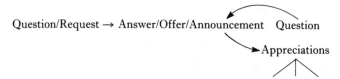

Question/Request → Answer/Offer/Announcement   Question

Appreciations

Here, then, as in the cases we have seen so far, the pronoun displays the speaker's understanding that the pair being returned to is, although possibly complete, not yet definitely closed. The pronoun helps to produce the feeling of "continuing" something that is still going on.

As I have formulated the pattern of return pop, it must be the case that the sequence which the pop returns to has not been closed down prior to the return pop. If a sequence has been closed down then a subsequent retrieval of some portion of the talk of that sequence is not a return pop. The exact structural status that such a move should have is unclear to me: but at any rate it is not a return pop, as I have defined that notion here.

Another example of a return pop, with pronoun, appears below.

```
 1. H.   Y'know w't I did las'ni://ght?
 2. N.   Wha:t,=
 3. H.   =Did a te:rrible thi:::://ng,
 4. N.   You called Si:m,
 5.            (0.4)
 6. H.   No:,
 7.           ( · )
 8. N.   What,
 9.           ( · )
10. H.   ·t·hhhh //Well I hed-
11. N.   You called Richard,=
12. ( )  =hh-hh=
```

13. H. =(h)y(h)Yea(h)h en I h(h)ung up w(h)u he a(h)ns//wer
14. N. Oh: Hyla why::::://::,
15. H. ·hhh=
16.   =W'first'v all I wasn'about t'spen'seventy five cents fer
17.   th(h)r(h)ee(h)mi(h)//nni(h)ts ·uh·eh=
18. N. Yeah,
19. N. =That's true,=
20. H. =·hihhh That's a l(h)otta money plus (·) uh then it's
21.   twunny five cents fer extra m:minute a(h)//fter that.
22. N. Yea:h,
23. H. =·hhhhh y//ihknow,
—→ 24. N. How do you know he answered

(HG:II:22–3)

This passage also illustrates long-distance pronominalization with a return pop. In this case, the sequence begins with H making a pre-announcement (lines 1 and 3), which N at first responds to with a clearance marker (*what*), but then guesses at once (*you called Sim*), gives up (*what*), then guesses at again (*you called Richard*), this time successfully. H's third-position response to the last guess indicates that it is correct, and goes on to add more news (line 13). This is the crucial line for the upcoming return pop. At line 14 N produces the first-pair part of a post-elaboration of line 13, and this gets a fairly lengthy answer from H (lines 16–23, with third position acceptances from N). At line 24, N returns to line 13 to do the first-pair part of another post-elaboration; this return contains a pronominal reference to Richard, the person last mentioned at line 13. The gap of ten lines does not cause N to use a full NP for the reference, as one would expect in traditional theories of anaphora, because the item being returned to is not yet closed (although it is possibly complete before the return). The pronoun at line 24 displays N's hearing of H's line 13 as not yet closed, and serves to help accomplish a "continuing" of that line.

The connection between returns to earlier adjacency pairs and long-distance pronominalization is not a new finding of this study. It was first noted in the natural language processing literature (Grosz 1977) that long-distance pronominalization was possible *iff* (if and only if) there were certain structural properties which held concerning the last mention of the item and the intervening material. Some of the structural properties which have been said to "induce" such long-distance pronominalization are given below:

1 In a situation of accomplishing a main goal by accomplishing smaller subgoals (e.g., as was the case, for example, in Grosz's work, building a pump), a return

to the main goal after work on a subgoal could be done with a pronoun. For example, Grosz found that speakers in her experiments could use *it* to refer to the pump as a whole (the object of the main goal) even if *it* had just been used to refer to a subpart of the pump. (Guindon 1986 reports similar results.)

2   If a speaker is interrupted, either by him/herself or by someone else, with a sequence started by what Schegloff and Sacks (1973) call a misplacement marker (for example, *by the way*), then the interrupted sequence can be returned to after the interruption is hearably complete using a pronoun. Reichman (1981) reports instances in which such an interruption goes on for 30 minutes and yet the interrupted sequence is picked up again with a pronoun.

These instances of long-distance pronominalization have been called "return pops" in the natural language processing literature, because the pronouns in these cases show a return to an ongoing concern after some stretch of talk in which the discussion is about something else. I have chosen to retain the term "return pop" for the sake of continuity with this previous work.

In my own work I have found a much wider range of situations in which a return pop can be done than had been previously identified. In essence, if there is a context in which there is a focal adjacency pair, with subsequent pairs tied to it (and to one another) by the adjacency-pair relations described earlier, then there can be a return pop to the focal pair. That is, the returning utterance must continue the returned-to sequence; if an utterance simply mentions a referent from a preceding adjacency pair, that is not sufficient grounds for calling the utterance a return pop. With the exception of same-gender environments (see section 3.4.2 for a discussion of return pops in same-gender environments), the basic pattern is for such return pops to be done with pronouns.

It should be noted at this point that a return pop is not *necessarily* a return to the most recent mention of the referent, as can be seen from the following passage, in which the return pop is to a mention other than the most recent:

```
 1. A.   Oh my mother wannduh know how's yer grandmother.
 2. B.   ·hhh Uh::, (0.3) I don'know I guess she's aw-she's
 3.      awright she went to the uh:: hhospital again tihda:y,
 4. A.   Mm-hm?
 5. B.   ·hh ·t! ·hh A:n:: I guess t'day wz d'day she's
 6.      supposetuh find out if she goes in ner not.=
 7. A.   =Oh. Oh::.
 8. B.   Becuz they're gonna do the operation on the teeuh duct.
 9.      -f//fi:rs]t.  Before they c'n do t//he cataracts.
10. A.   Mm-hm,
11. A.   Right.
```

```
12. A.   Yeah,
13. B.   ·hhh So I don'know I haven:'t yihknow, she wasn' home
14.      by the t-yihknow when I lef'fer school tihday. =
15. A.   =Mm hm,
16. B.   Tch! ·hh So uh I don't kno:w,
17.               (0.3)
18. B.   En: =
19. A.   = °M//hm
20. B.   Well my ant went with her anyway this time,
21. A.   Mm hm,
         [
22. B.   My mother didn't go.
23. A.   Mm hm,
→ 24. B. t! ·hhh But uh? I don'know=She probably haf to go
25.      in soo:n though.
```

(TG:3–4)

The return pop at line 24 is a return not to the last mention of the grandmother, which occurs at line 20, but to B's first round of answers at lines 2–6 (with A's continuers included).[11] Here again we see that the traditional theory of anaphora, which takes into account only the most recent mention of a referent, neglects a wide range of anaphoric patterns.

It is obviously crucial for this type of analysis that interactants, as well as analysts, be attuned to the differences between tying to the immediately prior talk and return pops. That is, it must be the case, if this analysis is to be at all meaningful, that recipients hear the difference between these two types of moves and, perhaps more importantly, that speakers produce their utterances so as to display whether they are of one or the other type. I would like to argue here that speakers do indeed build their utterances to display the level of structure at which they fit in: the "unmarked" level is the immediately preceding sequence; special techniques are used to indicate that the utterance returns to a superordinate adjacency pair.

The main technique that I have seen used by speakers to achieve the effect of a return pop is repetition of words used in the returned-to sequence/action. Examples of this design follow (the repeated words or phrases are enclosed in #s).

```
H.   Yea(h)h en I h(h)ung up w(h)u he a(h)nswer
     .
     .

     .
N.   How do you know he #answered#              [RETURN]
```

(HG:II:23)

H.   He-He went to: one mixer. et some,

.

.

.

H.   End he #went to one et some#   [RETURN]

(Friedell:9–10)

A.   Oh my mother wannduh know how's yer grandmother.
B.   ·hhh Uh::, (0.3) I don'know I guess she's aw- she's
     awright she went to the uh:: hhospital again tihda:y,
A.   Mm-hm?
B.   ·hh ·t! ·hh A:n:: I guess t'day wz d'day she's
     supposetuh find out if she goes in ner not.

.

.

.

B.   ·t! ·hhh But uh? #I don'know# = She probably haf to #go in#
     soo:n though.   [RETURN]

(TG:3–4)

H.   And there wz a ledder fr'm Da:ve.
     [repair sequence]
S.   What'd he haftuh say,

.

.

.

H.   He's:: (y'know) had two days of cla::sses 'n he #says#
     he's already behi:nd.   [RETURN]

(Friedell:8–12)

S.   Has he said anything about running into uh (·) Lawsin
     or (·) Da:ve?

.

.

.

H.   He did #run indoo#, (1.2) guy he'd known in the
     Philippines.   [RETURN]

(Friedell:10–11)

In each of these cases, exact lexical repetition is built into the utterance to indicate at what level it is to be heard. Ties to the immediately preceding adjacency pair are not as regularly designed to exhibit their ties overtly, hence my characterization of them as the "unmarked" move.

It should not be inferred from this claim about the design of return pops that all return pops are built with lexical repetition to display their structural position; some return pops do lack this feature. That is, it is not the case that lexical repetitions are required in all instances to "accomplish" a return pop. Passages in which return pops are accomplished without lexical repetition are given below.

```
 1. C.   He:y.   Where c'n I get a::, uh, 'member the old twenny
 2.      three Model T spring,
 3.          (0.5)
 4. C.   Backspring 't came up like that,
 5. C.   Dju know what I'm// talk] what I'm talkin a//bout,]
 6. M.   Ye:h,]
 7. M.   I thi]nk- I know whatchu mean,
 8. C.   Wh'r c'n I get o:ne.
 9.          (1.2)
10. G.   Just use a regular one.
11.          (0.7)
12. C.   Mmm I'd like t'get a, high one if I cou:ld.
13.          (0.7)
14. G.   I know uh-]
         [
15. M.   Lemme ask] a guy at work. He's gotta bunch a'
16.      old clu//nkers.
17. G.   Y'know Marlon Liddle?
18.          (0.2)
19. M.   Well I can't say they're ol' clunkers he's
20.       gotta Co:rd?
21.          (0.1)
22. M.   Two Co:rds,
23.          (1.0)
24. M.   And
         [
25. C.   Not original,
26. M.   Oh yes. Very origi(h)nal
27. C.   Oh::: reall//y?
28. M.   Yah.  Ve(h)ry origi(h)nal.
29. C.   °Awhhh are you shittin m//e?
30. M.   No I'm not.
31.          (0.8)
→ 32. C.   What's his name.
```

(AD:22)

In this passage, the return at line 32 to the utterance at lines 19–20 does not repeat any of the lexical items in the returned-to utterance.

```
 1. H.   = hhh Oh yih know w'n I wz talking
 2.      tuh Gra:ce.
```

```
 3.              (0.2)
 4. N.   °Gra//:ce,
 5. H.   Member Gra:ce?  my fren Gra//:ce,
 6. N.   Ye::ah.=
 7. H.   =·hhh Ay:::u::n, ·hhhh she has, these best
 8.      frien's.=
 9. N.   =Uh hu:h,
10.         (·)
11. H.   tha:t live in: Minneapolis. 'n they have a
12.      so:n.=
13. N.   Oh:.
         =[
14. H.   who's twunny:: four'r twunny fi//ve. Sumpn,
                                                         ]=
15. N.   Uh hu:h,
16. H.   =·pt·thhhh 'n he's in gra:d school i:n uhhh (·)
17.      bio chem °'r °something like tha:t,=
18. N.   =Sounds good,=
19. H.   =A:n ·hhhhhh  hnh-hnh //sounds kosher? ihhhh=
20. N.   °(shhounds ghhhood)
21. H.   A:n' he's coming ou:t. here,
22.         (0.3)
23. H.   January twunny seventh er // something.
24.       ·t·hhh
25. N.   Mmmm::::::: ::::::.
26. H.   =So: en she awready wrote him about
27.      me en evrythi//ing en she'd li:ke
28. N.   A w r i : : g h t.
29. H.   =(t') f//ix us u:p.
30. N.   Does he wanna meet you?
31.(H). °(So),
32.            (·)
33. N.   I mean d//z he wanna-
34. H.   Well he doesn' have too much've a
35.      choi(h)oice=
36. N.   =Oh yeh that's truhh!=
37. H.   =·i- ·u- ·e:hhh,
38.          ( · )
39. H.   ·u- ·uhhhh
           [
40. N.   ·uhnuhhhh
41.            (0.2)
42. N.   Well wt's (·) wt's he li://ke.
43. H.   ·hhhhhhhh a- ah: she says
```

(HG:II:19–21)

In this passage, line 42 is a second in a series of post-elaboration questions from N about H's announcement (at lines 26–9); the first post-elaboration question from N comes at line 30 (*Does he want to meet you?*). The two post-elaboration questions are thus tied to one another by the series relation, and are both tied to the announcement at line 26–9 by the post-elaboration relation. By this analysis, line 42 returns to the announcement adjacency pair, even though it bears a series relation to the first post-elaboration pair (one could say that the post-elaboration relation is the primary relation in this case). Note, however, that line 42 does not repeat any of the lexical items of the announcement (or of the first post-elaboration question, for that matter).

In both of these cases, return pops are done with pronouns but without lexical repetition. We will see later that lexical repetition in return pops is most often utilized in the environment of same-gender referents. I will postpone discussion of that fact until section 3.4.1. In any event, lexical repetition is not *required* in return pops.

Furthermore, the presence of a pronoun after a long gap does not necessarily indicate that a return pop has been done. This fact is illustrated by the following passage, in which a pronoun is used after a referential gap but its utterance is not a return pop:

```
  1. N.   Didn'you wanna rilly say hi:,=
  2. H.   =Ye:s, but ez soon ez he said hello I hung up.=
  3. N.   °Oh: : : : : : :,
             =[
  4. H.   So I don'know'f ah'll ge'charged the seventy
  5.         fi'c(hh)ents(h)'r not,=
  6. N.   =No I don't think you will but- (·) (you)
  7.         might git charged something,
  8.                         (0.3)
  9. H. ↓Oh:.=
 10. N.   =Unle:- you know w't you shoulda do::ne?=
 11. H.   =Call'the operator en said I gotta wrong//number,
 12. N.   u-Y:e:a::h,=
 13. H.   = ·hhh
 14.                    ( · )
 15. H.   Ye::h I din'think of it I wz too upset
→16.         about hearing his vhhoi(h)ce,=
```

                                            (HG:II:24)

Lines 15–16 contain a pronoun (*his voice*) which refers to a person last mentioned at line 2, a gap of thirteen lines; yet those lines are not a return to line 2 (or to any other line containing a mention of the relevant person). Rather, they tie, by the relation of post-expansion, to the immediately preceding adjacency pair (lines 10–12). I conclude from this example that a pronoun in and of itself does not "accomplish" a return pop, nor does its mere presence entail a return pop; while there is a close interaction between return pop and pronominalization, it is not a causal relation in either direction. They are independent facts which in some cases become intertwined.

Having looked at pronominalization in return pops, I would like to present a remarkable passage in which one of the participants displays her understanding of a return pop by willfully misinterpreting it as "tying" to the immediately preceding action (instead of back to an earlier pair) in order to make a little joke. With this action we see that *for the participants*, and not just for the analyst, there is a very real difference between an utterance that goes back to an immediately preceding adjacency pair and a return pop.[12]

1.	B.	Oh Sibbie's sistuh hadda ba:by bo:way.
2.	A.	Who?
3.	B.	Sibbie's sister.
4.	A.	Oh really?
5.	B.	Myeah,
6.	A.	°(That's nice.)
		[
7.	B.	She had it yestihday. Ten:: pou:nds.
8.	A.	°Je:sus Christ.
9.	B.	She ha//dda ho:(hh)rse hh hh
10.	A.	(ba:by.)
11.	B.	hhhuhh! ·hh (Guess) why-But theh-sh-I-She wz
12.		ovuh-She's lo:ng-She wz long ovuhdue.
13.	A.	Mmm.
14.	B.	And she, She had gai:ned about fawty pounds
15.		anyway. hh
16.		They said she was treme:ndous.
17.		(0.5)
→18.	B.	So I'm sure they're happy about that.
→19.	A.	Nyeh thet she's treme(h)ndous ·hhh

(TG:27)

At line 18 B does a return back to *Sibbie's sister had a baby boy* (line 1) with her *So I'm sure they're happy about that*, where *that* refers back to the fact of the sister having had a boy. At line 19, A on the other hand jokingly "misinterprets" B's utterance as an expansion on *They said she was tremendous* (line 16).[13] That A's utterance can come off as a little joke is a strong indication that some structural fact is being manipulated for humorous effects: the structural fact involved here is a return pop.

There appears to be still another structural situation in which a sequence is not yet closed and a pronoun is used. In this case, there is an adjacency pair which is tied-to by the following adjacency pair by one of the relations discussed above, which is in turn tied-to by the subsequent adjacency pair, which is in turn tied-to by the next adjacency pair, etc., in a "chaining" sort of pattern.[14] In fact, I will call this structure an *adjacency pair chain*. It seems that if there is a mention of a referent in the first adjacency pair of the chain and then a subsequent mention of that referent in a later pair in the chain (and no intervening mention of the referent), the subsequent mention is done with a pronoun. The speaker thereby displays an understanding that the sequence of the first adjacency pair is not yet closed, and in turn accomplishes the continuation of the sequence. An example of this pattern is given below.

```
 1. N.   Didn'you wanna rilly say hi:,=
 2. H.   =Ye:s, but ez soon ez he said hello I hung up.=
 3. N.   °Oh: : : : : : :,
            =[
 4. H.   So I don'know'f ah'll ge'charged the seventy
 5.        fi'c(hh)ents(h)'r not,=
 6. N.   =No I don't think you will but- (·) (you) might
 7.        git charged something,
 8.                      (0.3)
 9. H.   ↓Oh:.=
10. N.   =Unle:- you know w't you shoulda do::ne?=
11. H.   =Call'the operator en said I gotta wrong//number,
12. N.   u-Y:e:a::h,=
13. H.   = ·hhh
14.                   ( · )
15. H.   Ye::h I din'think of it I wz too upset about hearing his
16.        vhhoi(h)ce,=
17. N.   =Aw-:::::::,
```

(HG:II:24)

The structure of this passage can be roughly presented as follows:

pair 1
  pair 2
    pair 3
      pair 4

By using a pronoun in the first-pair part of the fourth adjacency pair, H shows that she is continuing a sequence which is still ongoing, even though she is not tying directly back to the pair in which the preceding mention of the referent occurred.

In all of the preceding discussion, I have presented cases in which it is a fairly straightforward matter, for the participants as well as for the analyst, that the sequence containing mention of the relevant referent is not yet closed. The pronoun in these cases is doing the routine work of showing that "nothing special" is being done. In the examples I will present now, on the other hand, the pronoun displays an interactional construction (or construal) of the sequence on the part of one participant which may not have been the construction of the other participant(s). These cases, in their different ways, fall into the category of reopening a sequence which might well have been thought closed by the other participants.

In the first subgroup of this type, material intervening between the utterance in question and the talk that it "ties" to is, by the use of the pronoun, shown to be an interruption, even if it was not heard as an interruption when it was first produced. The pronoun thus creates a retroactive construction of what might otherwise have been

    sequence 1   (closed)   sequence 2

as

    sequence 1 (not closed) interruption   seq 1 (continued)

The following passage exemplifies this use of pronominalization:

```
 1. C.   How's uh,
 2.              (0.7)
 3.(G.) ((clears throat))
 4. C.   Jimmy Linder.
 5.              (0.6)
 6. C.   He's-he's pm the Usac. (0.1) trail//isn'e?
 7. M.   No. He isn't runnin Usac, he runs, just, (0.2)
 8.      mainly uh, asphalt now, ·h//hh
 9. C.   °Oh r//'lly?
10. M.   =He does real well.
11.              (0.7)
12. G.   D'y' ever go down t'the S'ndusky track down,
13.        the asphalt,
14.(C.) (No,  )
         [
15. M.   I aven'been down there in years'n years.
16.      I don't care much fer
17.      asphalt. I like (     //        //    ).
```

18. C.   I'd rather=
19. C   = I'd rather watch the dirt track racing yeh, =
→ 20. C.   = How come he's r-what's:: is he tryina move up?

(AD:19–20)

Lines 1–10 in this passage are basically a question–answer pair (with two tries at the first-pair part, and notice that C's line 9 is overlapped by M's line 10). At line 10, then, the sequence is possibly complete. At line 12 G starts up another Q–A pair, but his first-pair part is not tied to the preceding pair by any of the relations discussed above; it is, in fact, a new sequence (although G's deliberate repeat of the word *asphalt* in line 12 is no doubt intended to show that line 12 is in some way related to what went before it), which closes down the previously only possibly complete sequence. At line 12, then, what we seem to have is:

sequence 1 (closed)   sequence 2

This interpretation of the talk is further reinforced by the uptake by M and C that G's first-pair part engenders: M and C both answer the question, thus indicating that they "buy into" the interpretation in which sequence 1 is closed. But at line 20 an interesting thing happens: C ties back to M's lines 7–8 by means of a post-elaboration relation, doing this with a pronoun. C thereby demonstrates that he understands sequence 1 to be not yet closed, which in turn shows that the Sundusky track adjacency pair is now to be heard as an *interruption* of a still-ongoing sequence, rather than as a new sequence following the close of the preceding sequence.

C's use of a pronoun at line 20 thus accomplishes a reinterpretation of the talk into:[15]

sequence 1 (not closed)   interruption   sequence 1 (continued)

In the second subgroup of the category of pronouns reopening sequences, we have the most extreme use of the pronoun in accomplishing an interactional feat. In this pattern, the sequence containing mentions of the relevant referent is in the process of being closed (by one of the closing mechanisms – either of the sequence or of the conversation – available to parties; see Schegloff and Sacks 1973 for a detailed discussion of these mechanisms) but is subsequently strikingly reopened when a pronominal reference to the relevant person occurs. An example of this pattern follows.

1. A.   Hello
2. B.   Is Jessie there?
3. A.   (No) Jessie's over et 'er gramma's fer a couple da:ys.
4. B.   A'right thankyou,

    5. A.   Yer wel:come?
    6. B.   Bye,
    7. A.   Dianne?
    8. B.   Yeah,
    9. A.   OH I THOUGHT that w'z you,
→ 10. A.   Uh-she's over et Gramma Lizie's fer a couple days.
   11. B.   Oh okay,

Notice that B initiates a closing of the conversation at line 4. A appears to accept the initiation at line 5, and B continues with the final closing at line 6; at this point we would expect A to produce a version of *bye* at line 7, after which both parties could conceivably hang up. As Schegloff and Sacks (1973: 317) note:

Once properly initiated, a closing section may contain nothing but a terminal exchange and accomplish a proper closing thereby. Thus, a proper closing can be accomplished by:

A: O.K.
B: O.K.
A: Bye Bye
B: Bye

For the conversation above to be properly closed, then, we would expect A to produce a final closing *bye*. Instead, she overlaps B's closing with an utterance that clearly calls for the conversation to be reopened (a first-pair part). B confirms the identification in the second-pair part (line 8). The conversation is now clearly open for both parties, and at line 10 A creates the additional reopening of the topical talk of the call (lines 2–3) by referring to the person mentioned in lines 2–3 with a pronoun. This is a striking instance of the use-determines-context mode of operating, inasmuch as A clearly accomplishes a reopening of the relevant sequence by using a pronominal form.

3.3.3   Full NPs used to display that a sequence is understood as closed

If pronouns are used to display a participant's understanding of a sequence as not yet closed, then it follows that full NPs are used to display an understanding of a sequence as closed.

   An example of a full NP being used to refer to a person last mentioned in a closed sequence is given in the following passage. The argument for viewing the relevant sequence as closed runs as follows: whenever a return pop is done, the material which is "popped over" is closed off.[16] In the following passage, the touched-off comment at lines 3–4 is closed by a return to the preceding pre-closing moves at lines 7–8 (M is about to leave the scene of the interaction). Notice that M's return pop at line 7 is signalled by *so anyway*, a common right-hand parenthesis device. When the person introduced in the now-closed touched-off comment is re-referenced at line 10, the reference is done with a full NP.

```
 1. M.   W'l (anyway listen) I gotta (go), I gotta(-) do
 2.       alotta studying
 3.                     (0.3)
 4. M.   Oh en Hillary said she'd call me if- she was
 5.       gonna go t'the library with me
 6.                     (0.9)
 7. M.   But- (0.1) I don't think she will
 8. M.   So ennyway (0.2) Tch.  I'm gonna go have these xeroxed
 9.       'n I'll come back inna little bit.
10.(M)   (·hhhh/hh)
11. R.   (Oka//y. Say]) hi t'Hillary for me.
12. S.   Okay.]
13. M.   Okay I will.
```

(SN-4:32)

Thus although the last reference to Hillary is only three lines away from the most recent mention, it is done with a full NP because of the structure of the material between these two mentions. Here again, the traditional theory of anaphora, which uses distance as the main criterion for anaphoric selection, turns out to neglect the fundamental issues faced by interactants when they choose among various ways of referring to people.

The following passage also illustrates the claim that return pops close off the material over which they pop.

```
 1. C.   He:y.  Where c'n I get a::, uh, 'member the old twenny
 2.       three Model T spring,
 3. ,                  (0.5)
 4. C.   Backspring 't came up like that,
 5. C.   Dju know what I'm// talk] what I'm talkin a//bout,]
 6. M.   Ye:h,]
 7. M.   I thi]nk- I know whatchu mean,
 8. C.   Wh'r c'n I get o:ne.
 9.                  (1.2)
10. G.   Just use a regular one.
11.                  (0.7)
12. C.   Mmm I'd like t'get a, high one if I cou:ld.
13.                  (0.7)
```

14. G.   I know uh-]
         [
15. M.   Lemme ask] a guy at work. He's gotta bunch a'
16.   old clu//nkers.
17. G.   Y'know Marlon Liddle?
18.   (0.2)
19. M.   Well I can't say they're ol' clunkers he's
20.   gotta Co:rd?
21.   (0.1)
22. M.   Two Co:rds,
23.   (1.0)
24. M.   And
         [
25. C.   Not original,
26. M.   Oh yes. Very origi(h)nal
27. C.   Oh::: reall//y?
28. M.   Yah. Ve(h)ry origi(h)nal.
29. C.   °Awhhh are you shittin m//e?
30. M.   No I'm not.
31.   (0.8)
32. C.   What's his name.

               [two stories intervene]

1. G.   Getta piano s//tring en cut 'er nipples off.]
2. C.   Jesus Chri:st Mi:ke?]
3. G.   hhh ·hhhh
4.   (0.5)
5. C.   Kesh! ·hh
6. G.   ·hhh hhhh!
7. C.   I gue::ss.
8.   (0.7)
9. G.   °That's pitiful.
10.   (1.0)
11. G.   Nah this Marlon Little's been building, roadsters,
12.   in th'str- considered street roadsters he builds.
13. C.   Nh.
14. G.   B'tche aftuh ra:ce 'em o//n the tra:ck]s (//).]
15. C.   Oh Little.]
16. C.   Little. Ou:t] et uh:m
17. M.   Yah right up, Por'//Clin' Roa:d.
18. C.   on Por'Clin' Road.
19. C.   Ye:h.
20. M.   He usetuh get dow//n there.
21. G.   He works over et the plant.He's (in the plant.)
22.   (0.7)

➝ 23. C.   Well I see I got my T bucket startih=
24. C.   =<u>We</u>ll I // didn't get it started I got it- I'm <u>ta:l</u>kin
25.   about it now I'm, tryina get things lined <u>up</u> for it.
     G.   ((clears throat))
             (1.2)
     M.   You wanna <u>mo:</u>del, what?
             (0.5)
     M.   Te//e?
     C.   <u>You</u> know what <u>you</u> know the kinda spring I'm talkin about.
             (0.3)
     C.   Th'muh-the <u>o</u>//ld model t]e//e-
     M.   Yah they're]=
     M.   =<u>They</u>'re
     C.   Yea//h.
     M.   They're a <u>hi:</u>gh <u>arch</u> spr//ing.
     C.   <u>High</u> arch spring.
     G.   <u>Oh</u>: jist across the back end?
         [
     C.   <u>Any</u>-<u>a</u>ny high arch.
     C.   °Yeh.
     C.   Yeh but-
         [
     G.   Well see (uhmy ex) father'n law down'n Port Clint'n <u>has</u>
         one thet's (not) <u>started.</u> He's, got the engine (out)
         'n <u>e</u>vrything.
             (0.5)
     G.   'N <u>eez</u> got- a spring thet comes, (0.7) way up, all-
         from one wheel t'the other.
     C.   Yeah, 't's right,
     G.   Big <u>hi:</u>gh en this is a twu: I <u>think</u> it's a twunny
         <u>seven</u>, 'r::
     C.   <u>We</u>://ll anyways if I cain' get it- I mean <u>I'm</u> just
         lookin fer so//methin.If ehy if it//'s <u>sub</u>stitute, yihkno:w,=
     G.   twenny ei//ght
     G.   But-
     G.   Uh: hh
     C.   =If I can' get that I'll just haftuh go, to a lower
         spring.// (   )
     M.   <u>You</u> c'n get'em <u>ma:</u>de.
     G.   S'm guys in <u>Bell</u>view bui//lt a <u>frame</u> (en it cost] em),
     C.   Yea:h, fer a fortune,]

       (another page of talk)

     M.   'F you needed a spring, yo//u wannid a certain type
         a' spring °you c'go out'n get it made.

    C.   Mm-hm?

⟶   C.   I heard <u>L</u>ittle wz makin um, was <u>m</u>akin <u>f</u>rames
       'n sendin 'm t'Cali<u>fo</u>rnia.

                                                         (AD:22)

This amazing passage consists essentially of four parts: C's request for information about a spring for his model T and the talk that engenders; two stories about men who own cars (one told by M and the other told by C); G's return to talking about Marlon Little (which picks up his question of line 16 of the first fragment); and C's return to talking about his model T and spring (at line 23 of the second fragment). C's return at line 23 to his much-previous talk about his model T pops over the Marlon Little sequence (which runs from line 11 to line 21 of the second fragment), and according to the pattern should close off this sequence. Indeed, the next mention of Little (in C's last utterance in the second fragment) is done with a full NP.[17]

In the following passage, a full NP is used after a sequence has come to a possible completion place, and a long lapse (5.0 seconds) has grown. Under these conditions, it is very likely that the participants will treat the relevant sequence as closed, since it has come to a possible completion place and all of the parties have "passed" on the opportunity to continue it. The full NP in the next passage thus signals the speaker's understanding that the relevant sequence had been closed.

    1. H.   Is//n't Peterson giving a, (·) <u>t</u>alk t'day,
    2. S.   Ih-
    3. S.   Yeah// I'm s'posetuh go to it,
    4. H.   °(et noon),
    5.   (0.6)
    6. H.   Et noon,
    7.   (0.2)
    8. S.   No.
    9. H.   O//h. When °izzit ( ).
  10. S.   It's the three uh'clock <u>sem</u>inar.
  11. H.   °Oh.
  12.   (0.2)
  13. S.   'n I have a <u>c</u>lass frm three tuh four en
  14.   that leaves me in the <u>F</u>rieze Buil<u>d</u>ing at four
  15.   te<u>:n</u>,
  16.   (0.7)
  17. S.   Trying to run through th'raiyn over tuh,
  18. H.   You c'd- (0.2) C'dn you <u>s</u>kip French one day?
  19.   (0.4)
  20. (S). °°(Yhe:::::h.)
  21.   (5.0)

⟶ 22. H. Dz Petersin have a copy'v the paper.th't
  23.   you c'd read.

(Friedell:15–16)

The sequence is possibly complete at line 20, and the feeling of completion is further reinforced by the long lapse at line 21. By line 22, then, H has every reason to expect that the sequence started at line 1 has been closed.

These are the major types of closed sequences followed by full NPs in my data. There are almost certainly other varieties which await description.

3.4 Anaphora in the environment of different-gender referents

It has often been proposed in the literature (see for example Givón 1983) that the appearance of a second referent in the discourse can cause the first referent to be referred to with a full NP. In the next two sections, I examine the patterns of anaphora associated with environments in which other referents are introduced. In the present section, I explore the anaphoric patterning within environments in which referents of different genders are mentioned.

The basic pattern presented in section 3.2 seems to hold for the environment of different-gender referents. The statement of this pattern is repeated here:

The first mention of a referent in a sequence is done with a full NP. After that, by using a pronoun the speaker displays an understanding that the sequence has not been closed down.

That is, pronominalization seems to be possible as long as the sequence containing mention of the appropriate referent is not yet closed; if this sequence has been closed, presumably a full NP is used.[18]

3.4.1 Pronominalization in a not-yet-closed sequence

As we saw in section 3.2.2 above, a sequence is most definitely not closed if a first-pair part has been produced and awaits its second-pair part. We thus find that if a person is mentioned in the first-pair part of an adjacency pair, even if there is a different-gender referent also present in that utterance, the basic pattern is for that person to be pronominalizable in the second-pair part. Examples of this pattern follow.

N. Y'do wunna see his forty four year o//l'?
H. hhhhhhh. =

H.   = ˙u:h-˙uh ˙k
     (·)
H.   ˙hhhh I c'n live without her, ˙hhhhhh

(HG:II:2)

In this example we have two referents, one male and one female, in a first-pair part of an adjacency pair; the female is referred to with a pronoun in the second-pair part.

Another example follows.

S.   Djiju tell her you had <u>s</u>ympathih-<u>sympathy</u> pai//ns
     for him?
( ) (̥heh)
M.   (h(h)h No.) I din' <u>t</u>ell her anyth(h)ing. ˙hhh

(SN-4:28)

Here again, we have a male referent and a female referent mentioned in the first-pair part; the female is pronominalized in the second-pair part.

The only other example of pronominalization in the environment of different-gender referents I have found is the following passage, in which (1) the first-pair part of a post-elaboration contains a pronominal reference to the (male) person mentioned in the tied-to core pair, and (2) the second-pair part of a return pop adjacency pair contains a pronominal reference to the (female) person mentioned in the returned-to pair:

```
 1. H.   =˙hhh Oh yih know w'n I wz talking
 2.       tuh Gra:ce.
 3.                (0.2)
 4. N.   °Gra//:ce,
 5. H.   Member Gra:ce?  my fren Gra//:ce,
 6. N.   Ye::ah.=
 7. H.   =˙hhh Ay:::u::n, ˙hhhh she has, these best
 8.       frien's.=
 9. N.   =Uh hu:h,
10.              ( )
11. H.   tha:t live in: Minneapolis. 'n they have a
12.       so:n.=
13. N.   Oh:.
           =[
14. H.   who's twunny:: four'r twunny fi//ve. Sumpn,
                                                    ]=
15. N.   Uh hu:h,
16. H.   =˙pt˙thhhh 'n he's in gra:d school i:n uhhh (·)
17.       bio chem °'r °something like tha:t,=
18. N.   =Sounds good,=
```

```
19. H.    =A:n'hhhhhh  hnh-hnh //sounds kosher? ihhhh=
20. N.    °(shhounds ghhhood)
21. H.    A:n' he's coming ou:t. here,
22.             (0.3)
23. H.    January twunny seventh er // something.
24.        ·t·hhh
25. N.    Mmmm::::::  :::::.
26. H.    =So: en she awready wrote him about
27.        me en evrythi//ing en she'd li:ke
28. N.    A w r i : : g h t.
29. H.    =(t') f//ix us u:p.
30. N.    Does he wanna meet you?
31.(H).   (°So),
32.             (·)
33. N.    I mean d//z he wanna-
34. H.    Well he doesn' have too much've a
35.        choi(h)oice=
36. N.    =Oh yeh that's truhh!=
37. H.    =·i- ·u- ·e:hhh,
38.            ( · )
39. H.    ·u- ·uhhhh
          [
40. N.    ·uhnuhhhh
41.            (0.2)
42. N.    Well wt's (·) wt's he li://ke.
→ 43. H.  ·hhhhhhhh a- ah: she says  (·) he y'know,
44.        th'las'time she saw him which wz (·) three years
45.        ago he wz pretty good looking
```

(HG:II:19–21)

The core pair in this fragment appears at lines 26–9 (an announcement and an assessment). The preceding lines provide leading-up, background information for the announcement (note N's anticipation of the announcement possibly by line 13, and certainly by line 15). Notice that two referents, one male and one female, are mentioned in the announcement of line 26. Lines 30–6 stand in a post-elaboration relation to the core pair, and, as we would expect from the basic pattern, a pronoun is used in the first-pair part of the post-elaboration to refer to one of the people mentioned in the core pair. The pronoun here displays N's understanding that the sequence is not yet closed and, in fact, that she is continuing it. At lines 37–40 we have laughter, which can indicate the end of a sequence. At line 40, then, the sequence is possibly over. At line 42, however, N continues the sequence with another post-elaboration (the second in a series with the first one) of the core pair. Since this post-elaboration returns to an earlier pair (and not to the immediately preceding pair), it is a return pop. In the first-pair part of this post-elaboration, N uses a pronoun to refer to the male mentioned in the core pair, again displaying her understanding that, while the sequence may have been *possibly* closed at line 40, it was not *definitely* closed, and she is continuing it. Then, at line 43 H uses a pronoun to refer to the female mentioned in the core pair, even though this person was not mentioned in the first-pair part of the current adjacency pair (and in fact had not been mentioned for eleven lines). In using this pronoun, H clearly exhibits an understanding that the sequence in which the core pair belongs is not yet closed. Of course, we can also say that by using a pronoun in this situation she *creates* an understanding for herself and her interlocutor that the relevant sequence was not closed.

We can conclude from these examples that the appearance of a *different*-gender referent does not alter the basic pattern of pronominalization established for the situation in which no "interfering" referents are mentioned.

I have no examples of full NPs used in the environment of different-gender referents, so no claims can be made about that portion of the pattern.

3.5 Anaphora in the environment of same-gender referents

In this section I examine the patterns of anaphora for the situation in which referents of the same gender are present. We will see in this discussion, as in the preceding section, that simple introduction of another referent does not necessarily produce "ambiguity"; it is the structural organization of the talk that determines what will count as "interfering" and what not.

The pattern for anaphora in the environment of same-gender referents seems to be something like the following. As we will see in Chapter 5, and following Reichman (1981), a discourse unit is in an *active* state if it is being tied-to by the current adjacency pair. For example, in the following passage, the first adjacency pair is *active* while the second pair is being produced:

```
1. M.   A:nd ( ) as far as that goes my father's on his
2.      honeymoon =
3.      = (y:ah ha ha°ha)
4. K.   (Oh::.)  Very nice =
5.      Where'd he go.
```

                                                                    (SN-4:10)

Even if the two pairs are not physically contiguous, as long as the second ties (in one of the relations we have described here) to the first — and this could be via a return pop to the first – then the first is in an active state while the second one is being produced.

Given those descriptions of active, the pattern for anaphora in the environment of same-gender referents can be stated as:

By using a pronoun when two referents of the same gender are present in the talk, the speaker displays to the hearer that the referent intended is to be found in an adjacency pair which is currently in an active state. If there are two referents of the same gender that are in pairs that could both be considered active (depending on what it is the speaker is doing), then the speaker will use other devices in addition to the pronoun (such as repetition of key words) to guide the recipient to the intended referent; if the speaker chooses (for whatever reason) not to use such devices, then a full NP will be used for the reference.

This pattern is examined in detail below.

3.5.1 Pronominalization for pairs in an active state

According to the pattern above, we should expect to find pronouns – perhaps in conjunction with other linguistic devices – used to perform references to persons mentioned in "tied-to" pairs, even if there are other referents of the same gender physically closer to the pronominal mentions.

The major subgroup of this class is return pops to one referent "over" a referent of the same gender. An illustration of this use of pronominalization follows.

```
 1. A.   Oh my mother wannduh know how's yer grandmother.
 2. B.   ·hhh Uh::, (0.3) I don'know I guess she's aw-she's
 3.      awright she went to the uh:: hhospital again tihda:y,
 4. A.   Mm-hm?
 5. B.   ·hh ·t! ·hh A:n:: I guess t'day wz d'day she's
 6.      supposetuh find out if she goes in ner not. =
 7. A.   =Oh. Oh::.
 8. B.   Becuz they're gonna do the operation on the teeuh duct.
 9.      -f//fi:rs]t.  Before they c'n do t//he cataracts.
10. A.   Mm-hm,
11. A.   Right.
12. A.   Yeah,
13. B.   ·hhh So I don'know I haven:'t yihknow, she wasn' home
14.      by the t-yihknow when I lef'fer school tihday. =
15. A.   =Mm hm,
16. B.   Tch! ·hh So uh I don't kno:w,
17.              (0.3)
18. B.   En: =
19. A.   = °M//hm
```

20. B.   Well my ant went with her anyway this time,
21. A.   Mm hm,
         [
22. B.   My mother didn't go.
23. A.   Mm hm,
24. B.   t! ·hhh But uh? I don'know=She probably haf to go
25.   in soo:n though.

                                                    (TG:3–4)

This passage consists basically of one question that receives three rounds of answers. The first round starts at line 2 and runs through line 9 (to line 12 if A's continuers are included); the second round begins at line 13 and runs through line 22 (line 23 if A's continuer is included); and the third round begins at line 24. The second and third round are tied to one another and to the first answer as members of a series, and they are all in a sense second-pair parts to the question of line 1. Notice that each round begins with *I don't know*. Now the critical pronoun that I am interested in here occurs at line 24 (*she probably have to go in soon though*): this pronoun unambiguously refers to the grandmother, and yet the nearest female referent in the passage is B's mother (mentioned at line 22), and in fact at line 20 another female referent (B's aunt) is mentioned. Why does B use a pronoun in this case, and how is it that the pronoun is unambiguous?

The answer to the first question is, in my opinion, directly tied to the answer to the second; that is, I am assuming that speakers use pronouns in same-gender environments whenever they can assume that the reference will be unambiguous. In other words, the claim is that speakers use pronouns whenever they feel they can "get away" with it. How is it, then, that a pronoun can be unambiguous in a same-gender environment? Quite simply, because of the structure of the talk, and the way the speakers display their understandings of this structure to one another.

In the passage at hand, B does two return pops (the second and third rounds of answers) to her first answer. Notice that each of these later answers displays its relation to the first answer by repeating exactly a phrase from the first answer – i.e. *I don't know*. B thus clearly indicates the structure of the talk she is producing by using the linguistic device of lexical repetition to mark which utterance she is tying to. The pop is in this sense accomplished, at least in part, by the repetition of guiding lexical items.

Now note that the pronoun I am focusing on here occurs in one of these return pop answers marked by *I don't know*. My claim about this pronoun is thus the following: a pronoun can be used in a same-gender environment (assuming for now that the referents are mentioned in different adjacency pairs) if it is clear which adjacency pair contains the antecedent mention of the referent – that is, which adjacency pair is being tied-to by the relevant utterance. The pronoun at line 24 is therefore unambiguous because the antecedent locus of the utterance at line 24 (and 25) is unambiguous – the utterance is clearly not tied to the immediately preceding talk but goes back to the answer started at line 2 (notice that lines 24–5 also repeat the phrase *go in* from line 6). And, as the only female referent mentioned in lines 2–12 is B's grandmother, B thus clearly displays that the grandmother is the intended referent of the pronoun. The return pop makes the returned-to item active, and closes the "popped-over" material, and the referential source of the pronoun lies in the returned-to material. What is critical here is the speaker's use of a linguistic device other than the anaphor itself to signal to the recipient the pair to which the utterance is to be tied.

Another similar example of return pop with pronoun in a same-gender environment appears below.

```
 1. N.  'n that made me feel good he-I guess he sees some
 2.        pretty bad ca:ses =
 3.            [intervening material]
 4.
 5. N.  Also he sid that (0.3) ·t what you ea:t, (0.2)
 6.        end how you wash yer face has nothing tih do with it,
 7.                    (0.8)
 8. H.  Yer kiddin//g.
 9. N.  nNo:,
10.                  (0.4)
11. N.  He says 't's all inside you it's 'n emotional
12.        thing'n, ·hhh e//n,

13.        [intervening challenges, supports of claims, assessments]

14. N.  I- c- I rilly b'lieve him cz another doctor tol' me that
15.      ↑too:,
16.          (0.4)
17. N.  A doctor et school tol' me the exac'same thing he said
18.        it's j's something new they're discoverin:g y'know hhh
19.        's like-
20.          ( )
21. H.  Mean I c'n eat all th' candy bars I want//nhhhow?hh
22. N.  ↑Yeah. And, en the fact that you, you feel gui:lty
23.        about eating them tha:t's what makes you break ou:t b'cuz
24.        it's (0.4) 't's all inside you, =
```

```
25. H.    = ·t ·hhh So people who've broken out ther just
26.       very emotional //peo(h)ple ha:h?
27. N.    hhhhh hih ·hhhh En ther worried a//bout it,
28. H.    ·ih ·uh ·eh ·eh ·e:h e//h eh
29. N.    ·hhh hh=
30. N.    =I don'know it sounds kinda cra:zy=
31. H.    = ·hh//hhhh
32. N.    bu:t
33. H.    =Jista liddle.
34.                    (·)
35. N.    We::ll,
36.                    (0.3)
```
——▶ 37. N.   He may me feel bet//ter anywa(h)y

                                            (HG:II:4–6)

Here again we have a case in which the pair that an utterance ties to is clearly signalled by the speaker, and this signalling makes the use of a pronoun unambiguous. In this passage, one male doctor is discussed, and N says, of him and what he said, *and that made me feel good.* Later, at lines 14–18, another male doctor is introduced, as a source of authority to support what the first doctor said. Between lines 19 and 36 no mention is made of either doctor, and then at line 37 we find a pronoun referring to the first doctor. Notice that in line 37 N repeats (although not exactly) the phrase used in line 1: *he made me feel better anyway.* The unambiguous pronominalization is thus possible at line 37 because N clearly signals her return to an earlier utterance (line 1) in which only one male referent was mentioned (the first doctor). The referent mentioned in lines 14–18 does not in any way compete for the anaphor.

This particular passage makes another critical point about the nature of anaphora in conversation: contrary to popular belief, the referent of a given pronoun is *not necessarily* the referent of the last use of that same pronoun. Recall that in the present example the most recently mentioned male referent (that is, before line 37) is the other doctor, *not* the real referent of the pronoun. It should be clear that we must look to the structure of the talk, and how interactants display their understandings of the structure, if we are to account for the anaphoric patterning in conversational discourse.

Another instance of return pop done with pronoun and repeated lexical items follows.

```
1. H.    And there wz a ledder fr'm Da:ve.

2.       [repair sequence]
```

```
 3. S.   What'd he haftuh say,

 4.      [3 pages of answers and more questions]

 5. S.   Has he said anything about running into uh (·)
 6.      Lawsin or (·) Da:ve?

 7.          [some answers to this question]
```

→
```
 8. H.   hhh En he did- run into a guy who wu- went tuh
 9.      highschool with me:, who's- (0.6) now a senior at Yale.
10.          (2.0)
11. S.   Highschool with you:.
12. H.   °Mm-hm,
13. S.   Same year 'r,
14. H.   One year behin//d me.
15. S.   Oh:.
16.          (5.0)
17. S.   Hm:.
18.          (0.7)
19. S.   B't nobody we know, (          ),
20. H.   No:.
21.          (0.4)
```
→
```
22. H.   He's:: (y'know) had two days of cla:sses'n he says
23.      he's already behi:nd.
```

(Friedell:8–12)

There are two male referents in this passage: Dave, who is first mentioned at line 1, and "a guy," who is first mentioned at line 8. According to traditional theories of anaphora, the pronoun at line 22 should thus be ambiguous, since there are two same-gender referents in close proximity to the pronoun. But once again we see the power of structural indicators for "disambiguating" anaphora: the pronoun in line 22 is part of an utterance which is a member of an answer series to the question posed by S at line 3; that is, line 22 pops right over the lines in which the other male referent is mentioned and picks out, by repeating the key word *say*, the item to which it is tied. The lexical repetition helps to accomplish a return pop to a specific point in the preceding talk, and this return pop allows the use of a pronoun to be unambiguous.

One last instance of this pattern is given below.

```
1. C.   I heard Little wz makin um, was makin frames'n
2.      sendin 'm t'California.
```

      3.   [2 pages of intervening talk]

      4. G.   That's all- he don't *have* any ki:ds, him en his wife
      5.   never had any kids'n,
      6. C.   ((clears throat))
      7. G.   (Whatta) they go:t y'know (   )
      8.   (0.5)
      9. C.   W'l,=
     10. G.   =I guess-
     11.   (0.7)
     12. C.   T!///Nah *he* helped,]
     13. G.   He's got] he's got eight *units* thet he rents ou:t 'n,
➡ 14. C.   He helped uh, *Merkie* build *his* T bucket up. I saw
     15.   *Merkie's* is un is a, *darn* nice lookin little bucket.
     16.   (1.0)
➡ 17. C.   En then I, ez I *heard* det- *you* know he built a *couple*
     18.   of'm up'n he usetuh build *frames* fer gu:ys=
     19. C.   'n then he, uh:: seh-uh sent a couple of'm t' Cali*for*nia.

                                                    (AD:32–4)

Using repetition of the words *heard, frames, send to California,* C signals a
return at lines 17–19 to the pair started at line 1, thereby "popping over"
mentions of a same-gender referent, Merkie. The pronoun in line 17 is
unambiguous, for the reason that C has clearly signalled the pair to which
the utterance is tied, and that pair includes mention of only one referent –
Little.

This pattern of repeating lexical items in a return pop in a same-gender
environment is a striking feature of the way interactants organize their talk
for their interlocutors. The crucial data are given below for emphasis (the
relevant lexical items are enclosed in #s):

      A.   Oh my mother wannduh know how's yer grandmother.
      B.   ·hhh Uh::, (0.3) #I don'know# I guess she's aw-she's awright
           she went to the uh:: hhospital again tihda:y,
      A.   Mm-hm?
      B.   ·hh ·t! ·hh A:n:: I guess t'day wz d'day she's
           supposetuh find out if she #goes in# ner not.

           .
           .
      B.   t! ·hhh But uh? #I don'know#=She probably haf to #go in#
           soo:n though.

                                                    (TG:3–4)

H.   And there wz a ledder fr'm Da:ve.

　　　[repair sequence]

S.   What'd he haftuh #say#,

　　　[3 pages of answers and more questions]

　．

　．

　．

H.   He's:: (y'know) had two days of cla:sses'n he #says# he's
　　　already behi:nd.

　　　　　　　　　　　　　　　　　　　　　　　　(Friedell:8–12)

S.   Has he said anything about #running into# uh (·)
　　　Lawsin or (·) Da:ve?

　．

　．

　．

H.   He did #run indoo#, (1.2) guy he'd know in the
　　　Philippines.

　．

　．

H.   hhh En he did-#run into# a guy who wu-went to highschool
　　　with me:,

　　　　　　　　　　　　　　　　　　　　　　　　(Friedell:10–11)

N.   'n that #made me feel good# he-I guess he sees some
　　　pretty bad ca:ses

　．

　．

　．

N.   We:::ll,
　　　　　(0.3)
N.   He #may me feel better# anywa(h)y

　　　　　　　　　　　　　　　　　　　　　　　　(HG:II:4–6)

C.   I #heard# Little wz makin um, was makin #frames# 'n
　　　#sendin 'm t'California#.

　．

　．

　．

C.   En then I, ez I #heard# det- you know he built a couple of
　　　'm up'n he usetuh build #frames# fer gu:ys=
C.   'n then he, uh:: seh-uh #sent a couple of'm t' California#.

　　　　　　　　　　　　　　　　　　　　　　　　(AD:32–4)

It is thus clear that speakers build their utterances to indicate the pair they are tied to; and the main technique used in this design is lexical repetition of the words used in the returned-to talk.

Another, less obvious technique that seems to be used in this design is the slight "hitch" that occurs in the returning utterance, that is, a small self-repair, a sound-stretch, an utterance internal pause, or a phrase such as *But uh* or *um* or *you know*. Such hitches are common in return pops, and could in a sense be a design feature of those moves; they need not be repetitions of hitches in the original utterance. Examples of this phenomenon are given below.[19]

    B.   t! ·hhh But uh? I don'know=She

    C.   En then I, ez I heard det-you know he built

    H.   He's:: (y'know) had two days of cla:sses

    H.   He did run indoo. (1.2) guy he'd known

    H.   ·hhh En he did- run into a guy who wu- went to highschool

    N.   We:::ll, (0.3) he may me feel better anywa(h)y

It is an intriguing possibility in same-gender environments that the hearer, upon hearing a pronoun, for example *he* in *He's you know had two days of classes*, does not immediately find the referent, since the speaker could in fact have produced further talk on the immediately preceding adjacency pair; rather, it could be the case that the recipient suspends resolution of the pronoun until the locus of "tying" of the entire utterance is clear (see Tyler and Marslen-Wilson 1982 for similar conclusions). This possibility is completely in keeping with the treatment of anaphora I am developing here; since it is the structural relation of the utterance to the preceding talk that determines patterns of anaphora, and not surface-given facts like topic continuity or referent ambiguity, the resolution of an anaphoric device must depend on the recipient's understanding of the particular structural pattern currently being developed. If the recipient cannot make a determination about the structural pattern at the time that the anaphoric device is used, then s/he may suspend resolution, or may make a tentative guess at the referent, until enough of the utterance has been produced to indicate the structural relation.

A second subgroup of the class of cases in which pronouns are used to refer to items in an *active* adjacency pair occurs when two referents of the same gender are mentioned in the same adjacency pair, or even in the same pair part. In this case, lexical repetition indicating the tied-to pair for an utterance is not sufficient, since the referents appear in the same pair. Here, lexical repetition combines with grammatical role continuity and lexical/semantic plausibility to create an utterance in which reference is unambiguous.

Consider, for example, the following passage, in which two same-gender referents are mentioned in one utterance, and in which, in a turn expansion of that utterance, pronouns are used to refer to them.

```
 1. H.   Dz Peterson have a copy'v the paper.th't you c'd read.
 2.          (1.2)
 3. S.   Evidently Wa:rd's not letting him, (0.6) talk
 4.       about what he wannid t'talk about,
 5.          (0.5)
 6. S.   M-he's making him talk about sumhing else th(h)et
 7.       evrybody's hea:rd.
```

S's turn at lines 3–4 contains references to Ward and to Peterson, and both are pronominalized in her turn expansion at lines 6–7. The pronouns are unambiguous in this case because of the semantic and grammatical structure of the utterance. That is, Ward has been established as the causer in a causative clause (line 3) while Peterson has been the causee. Furthermore, Peterson has been established as the agent of an event of talking. In lines 6–7 these semantic/grammatical roles are maintained: someone is causing someone else to be the agent of talking. Since the roles are explicitly maintained by the use of parallel phrases and structures (*letting him talk about* vs. *making him talk about*), the pronouns are unambiguous, inasmuch as they can be heard as referring to the entity that filled their slot in the preceding utterance. Here, as before, we see that pronominalization is possible in same-gender environments if other linguistic devices are utilized to guide the interpretation.

These data have significant implications for informationally based schemes that do not take structure into account. Prince's taxonomy for given and new information (Prince 1981), for example, would not be able to distinguish the pronominalizability of the referents in these cases, since in the instances above the referents would all be textually evoked. These data suggest, then, that further refinements of the given–new contrast (or of any other information-oriented terms) are in order to capture the complexity of this kind of anaphoric patterning.

3.5.2   Full NPs used when other linguistic devices are not used

It was claimed above that pronominalization is possible in the environment of same-gender referents if other linguistic devices besides the anaphor itself are used to guide the recipient to the intended referent. In cases where other devices are either not available or for some reason not used, full NPs will be used.

Below I present an instance in which a return pop over same-gender referents is done with a full NP, in contrast with the examples of return pops we saw in the preceding section. A full NP is used in this case, it is argued, because the returning utterance is not built (for whatever reason) to indicate what exactly is being returned to. The full NP makes the reference clear, given that there is no help from the structure of its utterance.

```
 1. C.   Keegan usetuh race uhr uh- er ih was um, (0.4)
 2.          usetuh run um,
 3.             (2.7)
 4. C.   Oh:: shit.
 5.          (0.4)
 6. C.   Uhm,
 7.          (0.4)
 8. C.   Fisher's car.
 9. M.    Three en//na quarter?
10. C.   Thr//ee enna quarter.
11. M.   Yeh,
12.          (1.0)
13. C.   (When I) wz foolin around.
14. G.    I usetuh go over there wih my cousin, °(when he
15.          had a car),
16.             (1.2)
17. G.    His name wz uh, Tucker.
18. G.    (They had a-) McGill from, °(Knotsville)
19. G.    Sam's from Bellview. He had a Oh Two. Ih wz a,
20.          modified.
21.          Six cylinder::?
22. M.   Oh yeah th//at's goin way ba:ck.
23. G.   °(That's a lo:ng time ago).
24. G.    Tha wz a lo:ng time a//go.
25. M.   Yeah.
26.          (1.0)
27. G.    I usetuh go over there the://n 'n, no:w, Rich Hawkins
28.          from Bellview drives one, fer some guys frm up't
29.          Bellview.
30. M.   ((clears throat))
```

```
31.          (0.4)
32. M.    Yah.
33. G.    He's my:: liddle sister's brother'n law.
34.          (0.5)
35. G.    He's a policem'n in Bellview b't he- (0.4) I guess
36.          he's not afraid t'drive a ca:r,
37.          (1.0)
38. G.    I d'know what they have tuh dri:ve I haven'even been
39.          over tuh see (im//lately)
40. M.    It's a pretty good ca:r.
41.          (4.2)
42. G.    Evry time I wen over there I froze m'nu:ts.
43.          (1.0)
44. M.    °hh hh//hh!
45. G.    You always go over en ni- nice in the afternoon en you
46.          go over there wi//th jus::]t shirtsleeves on 'er just a,
47.          short sleeve shirt'n fore the night is over yer
48.          freezin t'death.
49. M.    Yeah.]
50. G.    Yer not allowed t'dri:nk,
→ 51. M.    Hawkins the one thet hit Al last year over in
             Finley
```

(AD:17–19)

Although the exact structure of this passage is not clear to me, it is apparent that there are at least three male referents mentioned: Keegan (line 1), Tucker (line 17),[20] and Hawkins (line 27). Each of G's utterances seems to be a turn expansion of his own preceding turn, and so we seem to have something of a turn-chaining effect:

Keegan
   Tucker
      Hawkins

When M comes to produce his line 51, then, he must contend with the fact that there seems to be a chain of at least three male referents in the preceding talk. Now we can see that the lexical/semantic nature of M's line 51 could not distinguish what pair he means to be "tying" to: first, there is no repetition of lexical items from any of the preceding turns; and second, since all of the men mentioned in the fragment are race-car drivers in Ohio, hitting someone over in Finley is not a feature that distinguishes among them, especially since both Keegan and Hawkins have been associated with the agent role in events of driving (*Keegan used to race. . .* and *Rich Hawkins from Bellview drives one*). Given the structure of M's utterance at line 51,

then, and the structure of the preceding talk, a pronominal reference would
have been ambiguous; M thus uses a full NP.[21]

Another instance of full NP used in a return pop where no other linguistic
devices are used to guide the recipient to the intended referent follows.

```
 1. G.   hhOh my Go-o-d that's a, topnotch society over the:re,
 2. C.   eh heh heh
 3. M.   ((sniff//sniff))
 4. G.   eh-heh-heh eh(h) living aroun Bidwell en Greensprings
 5.      (with th(h)e // be(h)st) ·hhh hh
 6. M.   Yea:h.
 7. M.   We:ll,
 8. G.   They got nice ca:rs th.
 9.( )   °(Yeh)
10.             (3.0)
11. G.   ((clears throat))
12.             (0.5)
13. G.   Fraid tih g- (0.2) ((swallow)) go down there after
14.      da:rk, specially walking. hh
15.             (0.6)
16. C.   ((vl)) Ahhhhhhh
17.             (1.7)
18. C.   Well Doug isn't too bad a gu:y,
19. M.   No.
20. M.   His bro//ther's a] n-=
21. C.   He usetuh,]
22. M.   =(Yeh) brother's a pretty nice guy I// spoze
23.      probly the younger kids thet'r raisin hell over
24.      there,
25. C.   I::-
26.             (0.5)
27. C.   I know. I d- I know Dou:g en he isn't,
```

→

(AD:14–15)

Two male referents appear in this passage, Doug (line 18), and his brother
(line 22). At line 27, C does a return pop to line 18, but uses a full NP to
perform the reference. He uses a full NP here (i) because the utterance does
not indicate, through use of lexical repetition, what pair it is tying to, and
(ii) because neither of the male referents has been associated with the role of
being known by someone. The return pop by itself thus does not uniquely
select a given piece of talk to return to, and the reference must therefore be
done with a more explicit form than a pronoun.

The same situation holds if two referents of the same gender are
mentioned in the same utterance or adjacency pair: if there is no repetition

of lexical items, and if the semantic/grammatical roles associated with each referent provide no help, then a full NP will be used to perform the reference. Examples of this pattern follow.

> C. <u>He</u> helped uh, <u>Me</u>rkie build <u>his</u> T bucket up. I saw
> <u>Me</u>rkie's is un is a, <u>d</u>arn nice lookin little bucket.

(AD:30)

We can treat the second sentence as a turn expansion of the first sentence. In the first sentence, Little (*he*) is associated with the role of helping someone build something, while Merkie is associated with the role of building. That is, both referents are involved in an action process in the first sentence. The second sentence, on the other hand, says nothing about the process, or about the roles associated with the process; it is an assessment of the quality of the thing built. Given the lack of reference-helpful information gleanable from the utterance itself, a full NP is necessary to make the reference to Merkie successful.

Another example of this pattern is given below.

> 1. G. Yer not allowed t'dri:nk,
> 2. M. <u>H</u>awkins the one thet hit <u>A</u>l last <u>y</u>ear over in <u>F</u>inley
> 3.   en   4. (1.0)
> 5. M. flipped him 'n put <u>A</u>l^{22} in that bad <u>a</u>ccident.
> 6. G. Wzee
>   [
> 7. C. Oh rilly?
> 8. M. Yah. (2.0)
> 9. C. Al's a pretty damn good driver.

(AD:19)

In this fragment we have two male referents mentioned, Hawkins and Al. Both are known to be race-car drivers. Through M's talk at lines 2–5 we associate Hawkins with the agent role in a transitive event and Al with the patient role in that event. The reference I am focusing on here is the full NP in C's line 9. The claim being made about this full NP is that (1) C's utterance at line 9 does not repeat any of the lexical items from the preceding utterances, and (2) that utterance does not utilize the semantic/grammatical roles we have already associated with each referent (in fact, since both are drivers, either one could be a "pretty damn good driver"). The utterance itself does not help the recipient to pick out a unique referent, so to make the reference successful, C uses a full NP.

The passages presented in this section are the only examples of anaphora in the environment of same-gender referents that I found in my data.

Perhaps other patterns of anaphora will be uncovered in the future if a larger database is used.

3.6 Non-structural factors in anaphora

In the preceding sections of this chapter, we have seen the basic structural patterns which correlate with the distribution of anaphoric devices. In this section I would like to demonstrate that, while those patterns are basic, they are not always followed; that is, there are other, non-structural, factors which influence anaphora. These non-structural factors are rarely discussed in the literature on anaphora (Linde 1979 and Duranti 1984 are exceptions) and thus it is particularly important to examine them here.[23]

The non-structural factors I have isolated do not seem to form a coherent group; at least, at this point I don't see any common principle at work in them. I have therefore presented them below in a list format.

3.6.1 Disagreements

I found a few cases in which a referent was mentioned in a statement from one participant and was then mentioned again in a disagreement with that statement from the other participant; and this second mention was done with a full NP.

    R.   Those'r Alex's tanks weren't they?
    V.   Podn' me?
    R.   Weren't-didn' they belong tuh Al//ex?
➤ V.   No: Alex ha(s) no tanks Alex is tryintuh buy my tank

                                                       (US:24)

    C.   Oxfrey runnin-I heard Oxfrey gotta new ca:r.
    G.   Hawkins is ru//nnin,
➤ M.   Oxfrey's runnin the same car he run last year,

                                                       (AD:8)

    M.   Beer is even bedder den wine. Cause it give you more nutrition. Joe lives on beer,
    ( ) Hnh
➤ V.   No. Joe don' live on beer.// Joe lives on, Joe eats.

                                                       (US:90)

(Karen is co-present person)

    S.   You didn't come tuh talk tuh Karen?
               (0.4)
→ M.   No (0.2) Karen: (0.3)
→ M.   Karen'n I 're having a fight after she went out with
         Keith

                                                    (SN-4:4)

    (M) °(W't about Vinny. Did he talk about money?)
               (2.0)
→ V.   (B't) Vinny didn' talk no money wid me

     1. A.   Hello
     2. B.   Is Jessie there?
→ 3. A.   (No) Jessie's over et 'er gramma's fer a couple da:ys.
     4. B.   A'right thankyou,
     5. A.   Yer wel:come?
     6. B.   Bye,
     7. A.   Dianne?
     8. B.   Yeah,
     9. A.   OH I THOUGHT that w'z you.
    10. A.   Uh-she's over et Gramma Lizie's fer a couple days.
    11. B.   Oh okay,

                                                    (US:7–8)

In each of these examples, a statement or question is made by one speaker, which is then disagreed with by the other participant, and the references in both the statement/question and the disagreement are made with full NPs. This environment does not always induce the use of a full NP, however; a passage in which such a disagreement is made without a full NP is given below.

    C.   How's uh,
               (0.7)
    (G) ((cle//ars throat))
    C.   Jimmy Linder.
               (0.6)
    C.   He's he's pm the Usac. (0.1) trail//isn' he?
→ M.   No. He isn't runnin Usac, he runs, just, (0.2) mainly
         uh, asphalt now

                                                    (AD:19–20)

Notice in this passage, though, that C's statement (which becomes a question through the use of a tag) contains a pronoun and not a full NP; in the examples above, both parts – the statement/question and the disagreement – were done with full NPs (with the possible exception of the Vinny example). I don't have enough instances of this phenomenon to know if the presence of the full NP in the statement/question is crucial for the anaphoric form used in the disagreement.

An investigation of the interactive work performed by this anaphoric pattern is beyond the scope of this study. I point it out here because it appears to go against the pattern discussed above, which says that if there is a mention of a referent in an open sequence, then a pronoun can be used to do a next mention of that referent.

3.6.2   *know* + NP: Overt recognitionals

In one of the transcripts, I found several instance of a full NP being used when a pronoun would have been predicted by the patterns presented earlier in the grammatical context of *know* + NP, or in some related context in which the identity of a person is overtly displayed and negotiated. That is, instead of saying something like (*a*), speakers were often found to say something like (*b*):

(*a*)   A.   Mary is visiting me this week.
     B.   I know her.

(*b*)   A.   Mary is visiting me this week.
     B.   I know Mary.

In this pattern, a person is mentioned, either pronominally, or with a full NP, and then is mentioned again in the same sequence in an utterance (produced by any party) which stops the flow of talk to establish overtly that the person's identity is known. The latter mention is done with a full NP.

The exact nature and motivation of this pattern is not apparent to me at this time. I have given examples of the pattern below to demonstrate that it is a real pattern.

     V.   En <u>he</u> ro:de] away on his <u>bi</u>:cycle.
     M.   Didju find Jim?
            (0.5)
     V.   P(h)eddelin a<u>wa</u>y yuh see,=
➤ M.   =<u>Oh</u>:: dey-dih-yeh- I-I know dih cat,

                                               (US:2)

V. Yes, en I've seen the person before in your building
    becuss I cornered them once, thinking it was the
    father// of the son I wz// very mad.
J. e(hh)h!
→ J. Yeh. Uh-I dis wantuh know de person. That's all.

(US:43)

J. He-he-he's got- Yeh, yeh right! Jus// like that,
M. Hmmhh!
J. You know what I mean?
M. hh hh hih-hih-// hih-hih-hih
J. The hippy- type,
            (1.0)
→ J. ·hhh I know, he's onna top floor. I know dih guy

(US:66)

M. =No. I know (who) the guy. I know who d'//guy is.=
V. =Yeh.
V. He's ba::d.
    [
→ J. You know deh gu:y,
→ M. I know deh//guy.

(US:67)

D. ·hhh] Cathy McCo:n]nen. Tha:t's th'name I'm// tryina
    think of]=
C. Yeah, right.]
→ D. =Dju r'//member Ca:thy,]
C. Right. I: r'me]mber// her.]=
D. Yeah.]
C. =Right.

(Clacia:16)

P. =Mkke siz there wz a big fight down there las'night,
C. Oh rilly?
    (0.5)
P. With Keegan en, what. Paul// de Wa::ld?]
M. Paul de Wal]d. Guy out of,=
→ C. =De Wa:ld yeah I// (°know]//him.)[24]

(AD:8–9)

It seems that something about the environment of overtly discussing the
recognizability of a referent triggers the use of a full NP, even if the
conditions are such that the patterns given in preceding sections would
predict that a pronoun would be used.

3.6.3   Assessments

It has been noted by other researchers (for example, Duranti 1984) that a speaker's attitudes towards characters can be displayed through the anaphoric devices chosen to refer to those characters. In my own data I have found something similar, in that it seems that speakers tend to use full NPs to refer to people in an assessment situation, especially if the assessment is negative (negative affect). Examples of full NPs in assessments are given below. Notice that in each case we would have expected, on the basis of patterns discussed earlier, that a pronoun would have been used.

> V.   Don' haftuh be a value whenever I do anything not
>   fuh my wife, my wife wantstuh know why, I did (it).
>
> (US:11)

> S.   Just think what good training it-u Besides
>   Bill Steffie lives underneath th'm. (·) Pay
>   a hundrd'n fifty (h)en l(h)ive o(h)ver Bill Ste(h)ffie
>   ·hhhh
>
> (Friedell:24)

> M.   (He's got a m- He got a bicycle.)
> M.   (Y'get it) all the time. He always// bring his bicycle in en
>   outta the house.
> V.   En he does-
>   (0.7)
> V.   He does his // (   ).
> J.   (Onna) bicycle?
> M.   Ye//h.
> V.   Him.
>   (0.4)
> R.   Yeh.=
> V.   =Yih know,
> J.   But I cain't figyuh this guy with a bicycle
>
> (US:68)

It is not clear to me why assessments should "induce" the use of full NPs. Nonetheless, there seems to be a demonstrable pattern of this association in the data I have examined.

3.6.4   First mentions

We noted at the beginning of this chapter that the first mention of a referent in a sequence is done with a full NP. This pattern seems obvious enough.

In several instances in my conversational data, however, I found first mentions that were done with pronouns. These pronoun first mentions fell into one class: first mentions whose referents belonged to a general class of referents which was evoked by a frame (what Prince (1981) would call an inferrable).

This type of first mention with pronoun is something like the familiar frame-evoked definite NPs, as in

I read a really good book last night. *The author* was Dutch.

where *author* can be definite because of the mention of *book* – books tend to be associated with authors, pages, covers, pictures, etc.; the first mention of *author* is thus definite because of the frame associated with *book*.

In the instances of a frame-evoked pronoun first mention, the exact identity of the referent seems to be unimportant; in a somewhat paradoxical way, then, a pronoun is used when the recipient is incapable of identifying the specific referent, and is in fact not expected even to try to identify the referent. The *class* of referents is identifiable, however: and it is perhaps this identity which the recipient is being invited to "resolve" by the use of the pronoun (where all members of the class are seen as being basically the same). Examples of this phenomenon are given below.

```
B.   I'nna tell you on:e course.
           (0.5)
A.   (         )
     [
B.   The mah-      the mah:dern art. The twunnieth century a:rt
     there's about eight books,
A.   Mm//hm,
B.   En I wentuh buy a book the other day I //went ·hh went=
A.   (mm)
B.   =downtuh N.Y.U. tuh get it becuz it's the only place thet
     car//ries the book.
A.   Mmm
A.   Mmh
B.   Tch! En it wz twun::ty do::lliz.
A.   Oh my god.
           (0.4)
B.   Yeuh he- ez he wz handing me the book en he tol' me twunny
     dolliz
```

(TG:11–12)

In this passage, B is describing going to a bookstore to buy a book. Bookstores have associated with them people who tell you how much the books cost, and who take the money from you; hence, through the bookstore frame such entities as tellers or checkers are as a class identifiable, although no individual is directly identifiable through this frame. *He* in the last line of this example refers to some member of one of these classes (probably a clerk of some sort). His exact identity is utterly unimportant to the report that's being made – it is his identity as a member of a class of people who know things like the price of a particular book that is important here.

> B.   Ih wz, I don'know what I'm gunnuh do. hEn all the reading
>   is from this one b̲ook so f(h)ar the(h)t I haven' go(h)t!
> A.   hhhhhhhh!
> ➤ B.   ·hhhh So she tol' me of a place on Madison Avenue 'n Sevendy
>   Ninth Street. =
>
> (TG:13)

The university class is associated with several items – teacher, books, chairs, work, etc. In this example, we seem to have a first reference to the teacher made with a pronoun. Here again, the exact identity of the teacher is unimportant (and in fact unavailable to the recipient).

> N.   u-h↓O̲h::,
>   (·)
> H.   Bu:t
>   [
> N.   M̲y f: face hurts, =
> H.   = °W't-°
>   (·)
> ➤ H.   O̲h what'd he d̲o tih you.
>
> (HG:II:2)

It is shared knowledge for H and N that N has had an appointment to do something about her acne. *Face* here is thus a frame for dermatologist, so even though the exact identity of the dermatologist may be unknown to her, H can use a pronoun to refer to the dermatologist.

> N.   Eh l̲east you know he was h̲o:me, =
> H.   = nihh phhig thhea(h)l =
> N.   = on a // T̲hursday ni(h̲)ght (hn)
> ➤ H.   ·hihh (   ) ·hhhhh She coulda been ly(h)ing ri'next to
>   him
>
> (HG:II:24)

Although the pronoun in the last line of this passage could refer to a specific person known to both H and N, it is more likely that it is just one of a *class* of entities that is being referred to with the pronoun. If this ethnographic assumption is correct, then this passage is another instance in which a pronoun is used to refer to "just another" member of a category.

In each of the passages above, the pronoun in question could be replaced with a category label, such as clerk, doctor, or teacher. It is not clear to me why the speakers in these cases have chosen pronouns over category labels, but the pattern is real nonetheless.

3.6.5 Demarcating a new unit

We saw in earlier sections that it is the basic pattern in conversation for a reference to be done with a pronoun if the sequence containing mention of the relevant referent is not yet closed, even across adjacency-pair boundaries. There seem to be situations, however, in which the new adjacency pair is treated as a somewhat separate unit from the preceding material; the new unit can be demarcated with a pre-pre (*Can I ask you a question?*, *Let me tell you something*, etc.) or some other demarcating device. In addition, it seems that the reference in such a new unit can be made with a full NP instead of the expected pronoun.[25]

There are obvious weaknesses in this particular analysis. For one thing, it is not clear how one can provide independent support – aside from the full NP – that the unit being constructed is viewable as a new unit; after all, not every new adjacency pair starts with a full NP. What makes one pair a separate unit while another is to be considered a non-separate unit? For the instances in which another demarcating device besides the anaphoric form appears (a pre-pre, for example), the issue of circularity is less pressing; in other cases, even if the analysis is valid for the interactants, the issue of circularity might make it untestable and hence not very useful as a hypothesis about the world. In spite of these difficulties, however, I feel that this analysis is worth exploring.

Consider the following examples.

    V.   I getta attitude behind dis, Jim came in heuh befa:w,
→ M.   If I git into- y'know y'know now I'll tellyuh
         d'reason.
    V.   Jim came down tuh flash his money.
         (0.5)
    M.   If I // git into-
    V.   Y'know he got his income tax tuhday, ·hh en his wz,
         saying, c'mon// let's chip in fuh the boddle en he//
         threw money- hh

    M. °Yeh.
    M. Okay.
    R. Yeah.
    V. Now <u>he</u> threw money onna <u>ta:b</u>le.
    M. Who//o.
    J. He's no:t uh, he's not a <u>spend</u>thrift Jim.
→ M. Oh wuh lemme tellyuh now.
    M. I put fi'dolluhs'n Jim gave me (   )//
       yesterday I'm goin tuhnight. =
    V. Okay.
    M. =You'll have 'em- eh you'll have 'm tuhnight. Seven uh
       clock eight uh'clock I'll bring 'em over t'yer house.

                                           (US:76-77)

In this passage, the new unit is marked first with *now I'll tell you the reason*
and then with *Oh well let me tell you now* (a type of pre-pre, presumably),
and contains a full NP even though the unit is tied to an action in which the
same referent (Jim) is mentioned.

    M. A:nd ( ) as <u>f</u>ar as that goes my father's on his <u>ho</u>neymoon. =
       =yah ha:h hah
    K. Oh::. Very//nice Where'd he go.
    M. (Ye:ah)
    M. Well I hed <u>thought</u> he was going tuh Acapulco because it was
       such a hush hush se//cret where he'd be go:ing.
          ((door closing))
            (0.8)
    M. 'n I thought he didn' want anybody t'know er sum'ing
               (0.3)
    M. But
          (1.1)
    M. Indee:d he did <u>n</u>ot go t'Acapulco. Where did he go? He
       went up north.
         (0.5)
    M. They just, <u>t</u>ravelled up north end u::m,
         (0.5)
    M. I guess it's okay he's gonna be gone fer about another
       week
         (0.8)
    K. You <u>l</u>ike the <u>l</u>ady?
         (0.4)
    M. She's ni:ce. She's a nice lady.I <u>l</u>ike her.
         (0.3)
    K. Ah//hh
    M. Friendly.
         (1.0)

→ M.   B't-the <u>ba</u>:d thing was thet um::, (0.3) I hadtuh
    mo:ve my dad's furniture
            (0.7)

M.   from his place in Sanna Monica=I <u>h</u>ad tuh have
    <u>l</u>et the movers in (-) so.
            (0.7)

M.   Being <u>to</u>:tally drunk from that orgy on Saturday night
    I (h'd) t'get up (0.2) en go do:wn. (0.2) (Sanna)
    Monica with Hillery.

                                 (SN-4:10–11)

In this instance, M starts a new unit – a story – with *but the bad thing was that I had to move my dad's furniture*. Although this new unit contains a mention of a referent that had appeared in the preceding talk, the mention is done with a full NP because the beginning of a new unit is a place where full NPs can be used for otherwise retrievable referents. It is thus my claim that the motivation for using a full NP (*my dad*) is to display that the utterance produced here begins a new unit (a story that also serves as a complaint).

Another example of this pattern follows.

M.   So you dating Keith?
            (1.0)

K.   He's a friend.
            (0.5)

M.   What about that girl he use tuh go with fer so long

K.   <u>A</u>:lice?

K.   I//don't-] think (they're about),

M.   °myeh]
            (0.4)

M.   (Wha-?)

K.   I dunno where <u>s</u>he is but I-
            (0.9)

K.   <u>T</u>alks about her evry so often but I dunno where she <u>is</u>
            (0.5)

M.   <u>h</u>mh
            (0.2)

→ S.   <u>A</u>lice was stra:nge
            (0.3)

M.   Very o:dd.   She usetuh call herself a prostitute

                                (SN-4:29–30)

Here we have a return pop (S's last utterance, back to M's question *What about that girl he used to go with for so long?*) done with a full NP, even though there are no competing referents. Again, it is claimed that the unit started by S's utterance is displayed as separate from what has gone before.

```
    1. C.   Keegan still go out?
──▶ 2. M.   Keegan's
    3. M.   out there he's,
    4. M.   He run,
    5.          (0.5)
    6. M.   E://r he's uh::
    7. G.   Wuhyih mean my:,]
    8. G.   My//brother in law's out there,]
    9. M.   doin real good this year'n] M'Gilton's doin real
   10.      good
```

(AD:8)

In this passage, M uses a full NP in a second-pair part (line 2) even though we have seen that usually a pronoun is used in a second-pair part if the same referent is mentioned in the first-pair part. M's full NP here (i.e. *Keegan*) is used to begin a new unit – a list unit of who is around and doing well, which he then continues with *M'Gilton*. It is the separateness of M's unit (that is, that he is not answering C's question but also creating an internally complex unit on his own) that facilitates the use of a full NP here.

3.6.6   Replacing an action

In producing an utterance, a speaker may not be doing "more" of what has come before; s/he may be replacing, or producing a "substitute" for, an utterance which was previously produced. One way the speaker can show that the current utterance is a replacement for a previous utterance is to use the same anaphoric device that was used in that previous utterance; in other words, the speaker will not shift from a full NP to a pronoun, as we might expect from our structural rules, but will re-use the full NP. In addition, in most cases of replacing, other words beside the full NP will be re-used. These repeats of lexical items are another clue to the replacement nature of the utterance. Several examples of this replacement phenomenon are given below.

```
    V.   My wife//caught d'ki:d, =
    R.   Yeh.
    V.   lightin a fiyuh in Perry's celluh.  last year
         deh usetuh be a lotta fiyuhs in 666.
    V.   Remember?
──▶ V.   My wife caught th'kid lightin a fiyuh.
```

(US:4)

Here there is a nearly exact repeat of the utterance, done with the same anaphoric forms as in the original utterance. My claim here is that V's last utterance is intended to be a replacement for his first.

A common type of replacement occurs when an utterance is in overlap with someone else's talk, or is not sequentially implicative for the subsequent talk; in this case the utterance is treated by its speaker as if the other parties had not "heard" it and it is reproduced (possibly with some variation from the first try) using the anaphoric form used in the original utterance. An example of a speaker replacing a previous try with a new one is given below (the replacements occur at lines 11 and 13):

```
 1. M.   Keegan's
 2. M.   out there he's
 3. M.   He run,
 4.         (0.5)
 5. M.   E://r he's uh::
 6. G.   Wuhyih mean my:,]
 7. G.   My//brother in law's out there,]
 8. M.   doin real good this year'n] M'Gilton's
 9.        doin real good thi//s year,
10. C.   M'Gilton still there?=
11. G.   =hhHawki//ns
12. C.   Oxfrey runnin-I heard Oxfrey gotta new ca:r.
13. G.   Hawkins is runnin
```

(AD:8)

The next example represents an interesting switch on the part of the speaker from one perspective (Fillmore 1968) on an event to another perspective on that same event. That is, selling and buying are merely two sides of the same coin; in one, the person with the money appears grammatically in an oblique phrase, while in the other, that same person appears grammatically in a subject phrase. For whatever reason, in this instance M has chosen to replace the first utterance with a clause that treats the person with the money (Vinny) as the subject of the clause, rather than as an oblique phrase. The second sentence also replaces the imperative structure of the first sentence with a reassurance structure. The second sentence does not exactly redo the first sentence; rather, it is meant as a replacement for the first.

M.   =Th'barbuh pole sell tuh Vinny. Y'know- Vinny'll buy
     the barbuh pole.

(US:8)

The following passage further illustrates the use of full NP in accomplishing a replacement utterance.

> N.   I- c- I rilly b'lieve him cz another doctor tol'
>   me that ↓too:,
>   (0.4)
> N.   A doctor et school tol' me the exac'same thing he
>   said it's j's something new they're discoverin:g y'know
>   ·hhh 's like-
>
> (HG:II:5)

N first uses the phrase *another doctor* in *another doctor told me that too*. She then says *a doctor at school told me the exact same thing*; are we to infer from this that she has talked to two other doctors who told her the same thing? Clearly not. What we are meant to hear with N's *a doctor at school* utterance is a replacement of her earlier utterance *another doctor told me*, with some additional information (adding authority?) about the doctor and a re-characterization of what was told.

Two adjacent full NPs can thus be heard as coreferential, in a sense, if the second is designed to be a replacement for the first.

Another instance of a type of replacement is given below.

> M.   Hawkins the one thet hit Al last year over in Finley en,
>   (1.0)
> M.   flipped him 'n put Al in that bad accident.
>
> (AD:19)

In this passage, M gives a characterization of a complex event (someone getting hit in a racing accident), then goes on to give a detail of that event (someone getting flipped). He has thus moved from a general, higher-level view to an action-by-action view. In the next clause, however, he returns to the higher-level view to re-characterize the complex event (a bad accident). Since he returns to the general view after starting an action-by-action view, he can be heard to be replacing his original characterization of the general view with a new characterization (possibly to indicate that the accident was worse than was suggested by his first characterization). In this last clause he goes back to the full NP – further indication that he is replacing the first clause and not the second: the first contains a full NP while the second contains a pronoun, and since we have seen that a replacement utterance uses the same anaphoric form as the utterance it is replacing, the replacement (which uses a full NP) must in this case be replacing the clause with the full NP.

One final example of this phenomenon is given below.

    M.   Soon ez Sonny gets back frm the stoh. = Sonny's up et the stoh.
    J.   Uh hu//h?
       [
    M.   Wait'll he gets back.

                                           (US:45)

In this passage, the first sentence from M is "replaced" by the next two sentences from M: in the first sentence, the fact that Sonny is at the store is presupposed (you can't come back from someplace unless you're already there); in the replacement sentences, this presupposition is made explicit, and what had been done in one clause[26] is now broken up into two main clauses. The point to be made here is that M starts the replacement sentence with a full NP, even though the referent had just been mentioned in the immediately preceding clause.

3.6.7   Interim summary

We have seen in this section that, while structural factors establish the basic patterns of anaphora in conversation, they are not the only factors involved in any given choice of anaphoric device. That is, there are factors outside of sequences, adjacency pairs, return pops, etc. that influence which device will be selected in particular environments. These other factors represent a wide range of conditions, and it is not yet clear that there is any single feature which would hold them all together; nonetheless, they function for our purposes here as a group because they have the interesting effect of "inducing" the use of one anaphoric device in a structural environment in which we could have expected the other device. Thus, although structural properties are crucial in understanding the overall patterns of anaphora in conversation, our description would be misleading and incomplete if we ignored the influence of factors such as disagreements, assessments, and overt recognitionals.

3.7 Summary

In this chapter we identified and traced various patterns of anaphora in English conversations. It was claimed that as long as a sequence is not yet closed – if it is not a same-gender environment – a referent within that sequence could be mentioned using a pronoun (cf. Thavenius 1983). The methods by which speakers *create* the interpretation of a sequence being opened (or closed) were examined in relation to the general issue of anaphora.

In order to understand certain types of long-distance pronominalization and instances of pronominalization in the presence of same-gender referents, we identified a structural organization which was called *return pop*. With a return pop the speaker ties, not to the most recent adjacency pair, but to a pair that is superordinate to that; with this move, the intervening material is closed down. In most cases a return pop is done with a pronoun. These findings are in keeping with the work on anaphora done by researchers in natural language processing (Grosz 1977; Reichman 1981; Sidner 1983; Guindon 1986).

It was also shown that if two referents of the same gender are mentioned in the same sequence, then the device used for any next reference to one of them will be constrained by lexical and grammatical associations with them. In addition we saw that under certain conditions both same-gender referents could be realized by pronouns. This finding goes against the claims made by Reichman (1981) in her study of anaphora, in which she proposes that only one referent can be in high focus at any given time, and that a pronoun can only be used if its referent is currently in high focus, thereby disallowing the possibility of two non-coreferential pronouns in the same utterance.

Finally, in contrast with the proposals of most researchers, it was shown here that structural properties alone do not account for all of the patterns of anaphora exhibited in English conversations; environments such as disagreements, assessments, new units, and overt recognitionals are places where one type of anaphoric device is used when structurally we could have expected the other type.

4 Rhetorical structure analysis

The structure of expository prose has captured the interest of a wide range of disciplines, including rhetoric (Dillon 1981; Young *et al.* 1970; D'Angelo 1975; Winterowd 1975), cognitive psychology (van Dijk and Kintsch 1983; Meyer and Rice 1982; De Beaugrande 1980; Bransford 1979; Sanford and Garrod 1981; Britton and Black 1985), artificial intelligence (Alvarado 1986; Schank 1982; Brown 1985; McKeown 1982) and linguistics (Hinds 1979; Grimes 1975; Kamp 1981). While several of these studies have designed detailed and insightful notations for representing the hierarchical structure of expository prose (for example, the macrostructures of van Dijk and Kintsch 1983; the argument units of Alvarado 1986; the rhetorical schemas of McKeown 1982; the conceptual graph structures of Graesser and Goodman 1985; the structures of Meyer 1985), none of them provides all that is needed for an in-depth exploration of anaphora. For this study it was necessary to have a notation with the following characteristics:

Ability to represent a fairly complete range of argumentation relations. A model was needed that would provide relations like evidence, background, summary, justification.

Flexibility of combination. Given the range of texts examined (obituaries, biography, announcements, feature articles), it was important that the basic units be combinable in a relatively free way, rather than tightly constrained, as in a grammar.[1]

Ability to represent texturing. It is now widely recognized that not all parts of a text hold the same communicative importance – some information is presented as central to the goals of the text and some as peripheral (Hopper and Thompson 1980; Grimes 1975). It was critical that the model be capable of capturing in some explicit way this distinction between central and peripheral for each basic unit.

The system I found that satisfied these conditions was rhetorical structure analysis (Mann *et al.* 1982), based in part on Grimes 1975 and McKeown 1982.[2] Rhetorical structure analysis forms the basis of the analyses in

Chapter 5, and is described in some detail below. This approach is not yet well developed, and the following discussion is offered only as a first approximation to what such a framework would look like in its complete form.

4.1   Rhetorical structure concepts

The basic assumption underlying rhetorical structure analysis is that texts are not merely strings of clauses but are instead groups of hierarchically organized clauses which bear various informational and interactional relations to one another (cf. van Dijk and Kintsch 1983; Mandler and Johnson 1977; Dillon 1981; Meyer and Rice 1982). The model thus has in its apparatus a basic unit – the proposition – and a class of text-structures which describe the structures which the proposition display. I will present each of these components in turn.

4.1.1   Propositions

The smallest unit of text in this framework is called the *proposition*. A proposition is more abstract than a clause or sentence, and is intended to represent the smallest unit that enters into informational and/or interactional relationships with other parts of the text. The propositions of rhetorical structure analysis are not equivalent to the propositions of Kintsch's work (Kintsch 1974); they are closer to the statement nodes of Graesser and Goodman (1985) or the idea units of Mayer (1985). They are often equivalent to clauses but need not be; for example, relative clauses are treated as belonging with their modified clause in one proposition, rather than as their own propositions. The same is true for most complement clauses. The motivation behind this treatment of relative and complement clauses is the belief that such clauses tend to be governed by principles of grammar rather than by principles of discourse, and hence are less closely involved with principles of organization. The use of an abstract unit is not necessary for the application of the rest of the model, however; clauses could be used just as effectively.[3]

4.1.2   R-structures

We have seen that, within this model of discourse, texts are treated as hierarchically organized groups of propositions (or clauses). The groups into which the propositions are arranged are represented here by what are called *R-structures* (which stands for rhetorical structures). Most R-structures consist of a core portion and an ancillary portion, called the *nucleus* and *adjunct* respectively. The nucleus realizes the main goals of the writer, and the adjunct provides supplementing information for the material in the nucleus. Not all R-structures have this internal make-up, however; there are a few that consist only of nuclei (the List structure, for example), and at least one that has a nucleus and several adjuncts. R-structures are drawn with their label at the top (such as "Conditional"), and several lines descending from the top. The nucleus is represented in the diagrams with a straight vertical line coming down from the R-structure label, and the adjunct is represented with an arcing line coming out of the bottom of the nucleus line. The arcing line is labeled with the name of the *relation* which holds between the nucleus and the adjunct (reason, for example). This relation label is usually identical to the label for the R-structure itself; in some cases, however, the relation carries a different label from that of the structure. Table 4.1 lists all the R-structures used in this study and their internal structure.[4]

Table 4.1 *R-structures*

R-structure name	Internal structure
Issue	One nucleus, three optional adjuncts
Conditional	One nucleus, one adjunct
Circumstance	One nucleus, one adjunct
List	Unlimited number of nuclei, no adjuncts
Narrate	Unlimited number of nuclei, no adjuncts
Reason	One nucleus, one adjunct
Concession	One nucleus, one adjunct
Opposition	One nucleus, one adjunct
Purpose	One nucleus, one adjunct
Response	One nucleus, one adjunct
Contrast	Unlimited number of nuclei, or: one nucleus, one adjunct

Each unit can be realized either by terminal nodes – i.e. propositions – or by another R-structure. That is, R-structures build upon one another to construct the entire text. We therefore have simple R-structures, with all of their slots (nuclei and adjuncts) realized by propositions, and complex R-structures, which have at least one of their slots realized by an embedded R-structure. The notion of embedding[5] will be crucial in the discussion of anaphora and text-structure in Chapter 5.

The R-structures are described and illustrated below.

4.1.2.1   Issue

The Issue structure[6] is the most powerful organizing unit within the model, and usually occurs as the top-most unit of the text. The Issue structure presents a claim, and provides at least one of three types of supplemental material: details about the claim (called an *elaboration* adjunct); evidence in support of the claim (called an *evidence* adjunct); and background information for the claim (called a *background* adjunct).[7] For example, a typical structure for a short obituary is to present the news of the death (the nucleus of the Issue structure), plus some details about the circumstances of the death (an elaboration adjunct on the nucleus), and then to give background information about the deceased which makes the death "newsworthy" (a background adjunct). The structure of such a text would be diagrammed in the figure below.

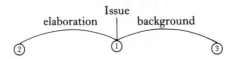

A real example of the Issue structure is given below (the propositions are numbered so that the diagram can be more easily followed).

(1)   Naftaly S. Glasman has been appointed dean of the Graduate School of Education at Santa Barbara.

(2)   A professor of education, Glasman has been a member of the UCSB faculty since 1968 and acting dean of the School of Education since January.

(3)   He has served as chairman of the faculty committee on effective teaching

(4)   and has chaired and organized two national conferences on effective teaching.

(5)   Recently he was appointed to a statewide committee on the professions, as part of the UC graduate student affirmative action program. (*University Bulletin*, June 28, 1980)

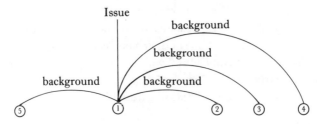

The entire text can be represented with an Issue structure. The first proposition is the nucleus of the text, in that it provides the news which the text is intended to convey. The other four propositions are background adjuncts – they do not provide evidence for the claim "X has been appointed dean," nor do they provide details about the appointment; rather they provide background information which elucidates the claim. This fact is represented by four separate background adjuncts.[8]

The Issue structure thus has a unique internal structure (one nucleus and many adjuncts) and often occupies a unique place in the structure of a text – the topmost node.

4.1.2.2 List

The List structure is another of the most prevalent and powerful organizing units. It has an unlimited number of nuclei (as many as there are items in the list) and no adjuncts. Each item is seen as a member of the List unit, rather than as a separate adjunct, because of the impression they create of each being one in a series (hence they are each only part of a larger unit). In addition, the members of the list are presented as equal. Syntactic parallelism is extremely common in this structure.[9]

(1) He knew his Rousseau;
(2) he knew his Voltaire;
(3) he even knew his President de Brosses! (Leon Edel, *Bloomsbury: A House of Lions*, p. 39)

(1) He spoke continuously for three hours from a platform in Memorial Park during Claremont's 1979 Fourth of July festivities.
(2) The next year, at the same rostrum, he stretched it out four hours.
(3) The next Fourth of July, on a similar platform half a continent away, he talked nearly six hours. (*Los Angeles Times*, July 3, 1983)

In these examples, each piece is one in a series. Note the strong parallelism in syntactic and lexical structure within each List structure.

4.1.2.3   Narrate

Narrate is the third and last of the higher-level R-structures. Like the List structure, Narrate has an unlimited number of nuclei and no adjuncts. Within this structure, however, each piece describes a temporally situated action which follows the last action in the temporal sequence. This structure allows a short narrative to be part of an expository text

(1)   Word reaches him that his masters . . . have changed their minds yet again on a major issue.

(2)   Rochac dictates a new strategy. . . .

(3)   One more crisis overcome, he cuts the tension with his favorite catchphrase. (*People*, May 26, 1984)

(1)   Within seconds, Chico has spotted the van.

(2)   He is walking toward it, crying, "Where is my little buddy? Where's my little Trevor?"

(3)   Soon the derelict is hugging and kissing the boy. (*People*, March 26, 1984)

4.1.2.4   Reason

Unlike the preceding structures, the Reason structure usually occurs at the lower levels of the text, and often is realized directly by terminal nodes (propositions). This R-structure has a nucleus which makes a statement about something and an adjunct which provides the reason for that statement (either the reason for making it or the reason for it being so). Examples of the Reason structure appear below.

(1)   Last year the Irish government boycotted the celebration

(2)   because the grand marshal was IRA fundraiser Michael Flannery. (*People*, March 19, 1984)

Here the second proposition provides the reason for the situation described by the first.

(1)   Buy only enough for immediate use
(2)   as they spoil rather easily. (*Joy of Cooking*, cited in Mann *et al.* 1982)

Reason

Here again, the second proposition provides the reason for doing the action described in the first.

4.1.2.5   Circumstance

The Circumstance structure is another of the lower-level structures. In it, the nucleus describes a situation and the adjunct gives information about the circumstances under which the situation occurred (or will occur). Circumstance differs from the background relation, in that Circumstance immediately situates a process in time or space, while background gives information of various types which helps the reader understand the nuclear material. Examples of the Circumstance structure are given below.

(1)   When Victoria came to the throne,
(2)   he was living in a comfortable house in or near Tavistock Square. (*A House of Lions*, p. 19)

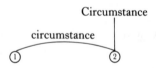

Circumstance

circumstance

In this passage, the first proposition provides the circumstances and the second provides the situation. The first proposition is thus diagrammed as the adjunct of the structure, and the second is the nucleus.

(1)   When we visited our in-laws in Florida a couple of years ago,
(2)   a sign flapped on the front door that read. . . . (Erma Bombeck column, cited in Mann *et al.* 1982)

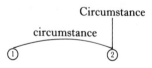

Circumstance

circumstance

Here again, the first proposition is the adjunct of the Circumstance structure and the second proposition is the nucleus of the structure.

4.1.2.6 *Conditional*

The Conditional structure is very similar to the Circumstance structure: the adjunct provides the conditions under which the nucleus holds. The conditions in this case are usually hypothetical.

(1)   If Judy Blume were the protagonist of a novel,
(2)   she'd be pretty hard to stomach. (*People*, March 19, 1984)

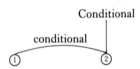

In this piece of text, the first proposition is the adjunct stating the conditions under which the nucleus, realized by the second proposition, holds.

(1)   If something like this happens twice to the same woman,
(2)   it is time for her to find what [game] she has been playing. (E. Berne, *Games People Play*)

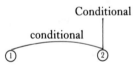

Again, the first proposition is the adjunct and the second is the nucleus.

4.1.2.7 *Response*

In the Response structure, a problem or question is posed by the writer which is then responded to with some sort of solution or answer. In this structure, the answer is the nucleus and the question is the adjunct.

(1)   What if you're having to clean floppy drive heads too often?
(2)   Ask for SYNCOM diskettes. (*Byte* magazine, cited in Mann *et al.* 1982)

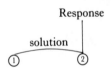

The first proposition, the question, is the adjunct and the second proposition, the answer, is the nucleus.

(1)   What was this carapace which Leonard Woolf carried for seventy years . . . ?

(2)   He had above all an unusual capacity to control his feelings. (*A House of Lions*, p. 24)

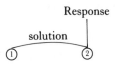

4.1.2.8.   *Purpose*

As one would expect, the Purpose structure has a nucleus which describes some situation and an adjunct which describes the purpose which that situation is intended to fulfill.

(1)   Allow the terrapin to cool on its back

(2)   in order to trap the juices. (*Joy of Cooking*, cited in Mann *et al.* 1982)

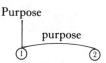

(1)   Ana Maria stayed,

(2)   to work within the system. (*People*, March 26, 1984)

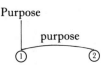

In both of these examples the purpose adjunct occurs as the second proposition; the first proposition is the nucleus.

4.1.2.9   *Opposition*

With the Opposition structure, the writer presents two sides of a situation – one, the adjunct, is the side not sympathized with, and the other, the nucleus, is the side the writer really supports. This structure is often realized with the phrase *rather than*, or with the pattern "not X but Y."

(1)   Rather than winning them with arms,

(2)   we'd win them by our example (Letter to the editor of the *Christian Science Monitor*, cited in Mann *et al.* 1982)

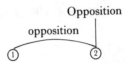

(1)   But I don't think endorsing a specific nuclear freeze proposal is appropriate for CCC.
(2)   We should limit our involvement in defense and weaponry to matters of process. (Common Cause, *The Insider*, July 1982)

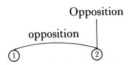

4.1.2.10   Concession

The Concession structure differs from the Opposition structure in that it offers material in the adjunct which is possibly at odds with the material in the nucleus, and concedes that this conflicting state may hold. The writer thus does not, in this case, reject the validity of the material in the adjunct.

(1)   While FitzGerald doesn't have a quarrel with this year's grand marshal . . .
(2)   he is annoyed by the selection of IRA fugitive Michael O'Rourke. (*People*, March 19, 1984)

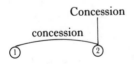

(1)   While we believe the distribution of this information is of benefit to our subscribers,
(2)   we firmly respect the wishes of any subscriber who does not want to receive such promotional literature. (Note to subscribers of *Byte* magazine, cited in Mann *et al.* 1982)

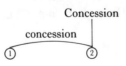

In each case, the conceding adjunct is given in the first proposition and the nucleus material is given in the second proposition.

4.1.2.11   *Contrast*

The Contrast structure comes in two forms: in the first, all the contrasted items are of equal status in the presentation of the material; in the second, one item is being contrasted with another item, where the latter has more focal status than the former. In the first case, the Contrast structure consists of multiple nuclei, in the second case of a nucleus and an adjunct. Examples of the multiple-nuclei Contrast are given below.

(1)   One was deep and manly;
(2)   the other was tiny and a squeak. (*A House of Lions*, p. 34)

Contrast

(1)   One airport source said the gunmen may have gone to a nearby Shiite shanty-town called Hayya Seloum,
(2)   but authorities weren't sure what had happened to them. (News item in the UCLA *Daily Bruin*, cited in Thompson, class lectures)

Contrast

4.1.3   The Joint

The Joint schema is similar to the list structure in that it is multi-nucleid, but is different from List in that the pieces are not presented as members of a series. The pieces of a Joint structure simply work together to realize whatever R-structure they are embedded in. Any R-structure can have either its nucleus or its adjunct realized with a Joint schema. The effect is something like rhetorical conjunction (which is not always equivalent to syntactic conjunction). An example of the Joint schema is given below.

(1)   I personally favor the initiative
(2)   and ardently support disarmament negotiations. (Common Cause, *The Insider*, July 1982)

Joint

4.1.4   Floating relations

In addition to the relations which exist within R-structures – for example, Reason, Circumstance – there are *floating relations* which are not associated with any particular R-structure. These floating relations can occur between a proposition of any R-structure and another proposition. The floating relations used in this study are Summary, Conclusion, Result, and Assessment. A brief description of each follows.

The *Summary* relation provides a summary of the material to which it is scoped. The summarizing material can have any R-structure as its realization, and can be as simple as a single proposition or as complex as a multi-layered embedding.

[at the end of a lengthy article entitled "'No First Use' of Nuclear Weapons"]
The adoption of a no-first-use policy would have profound consequences. In contrast to arms-control measures, which rarely constrain the actual use of weapons, a no-first-use policy would transform the conceptual foundation on which military strategy and planning rest. . . . (*Scientific American*, March 1984)

The structure of this passage in relation to the text it summarizes can be represented as follows:

The *Conclusion* relation provides information which is inferred from other facts already presented (by whatever method of reasoning the author cares to use, not necessarily deduction). It thus differs from the Summary relation in that it offers information which has not yet been brought up, while the Summary relation merely repeats in capsule form what has already been presented.

[at the end of a book review]
All in all, given the difficulty in keeping up with even basic research of the caliber that these authors produce, it is hard to see why the editors bothered publishing this collection. (*Language* 60(1), 1984)

The structure of the relationship between this passage and the material it draws its inference from is given below.

The *Result* relation describes circumstances which are the result of some set of other circumstances.

(1)   For years Leonard knew how *not to feel* – how to distance himself from intimacy.

(2)   This made for an uneasy calm. (*A House of Lions*, p. 24)

The *Assessment* relation provides the author's comments and evaluations on a portion of text. In some instances an Assessment looks very much like a Conclusion, since the author uses a group of propositions on which to base an inferenced statement; in the case of an Assessment, however, the statement is clearly evaluative (either positive or negative), while in the case of a Conclusion the statement can be simply informational. An example of the Assessment relation follows.

"When I left for St. Paul's in 1894," he wrote with a note of distinct pride years later, "the atmosphere had changed from that of a sordid brothel to that more appropriate to fifty fairly happy small boys under the age of fourteen." Leonard was a reformer from the first. (*A House of Lions*, p. 23)

In this passage the line *Leonard was a reformer from the first* is in an Assessment relation to the material that precedes it. This relation can be diagrammed in the following way.

4.1.5   Embedding

The examples given above have illustrated R-structures using simple data – that is, structures realized by terminal nodes. In this section, we shall examine some more complex data – texts that exhibit embedding.

Any of the pieces of an R-structure can be realized by another R-structure; that is, either the nucleus or the adjunct (or any of the nuclei in a multi-nuclei structure) can be realized not directly by a proposition but textually by an embedded R-structure. Short examples of embedded structures appear below.

(1)   I personally favor the initiative

(2)   and ardently support disarmament negotiations to reduce the risk of war.

(3)   But I don't think endorsing a specific nuclear freeze proposal is appropriate for CCC.

(4) We should limit our involvement in defense and weaponry to matters of process. (Common Cause, *The Insider*, July 1982)

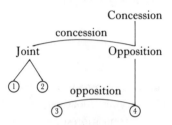

The structure which encompasses this entire chunk of text is a Concession structure. The Concession structure displays embeddings at both slots; its nucleus is realized by an Opposition structure, and its adjunct is realized by a Joint structure. The Joint structure is realized directly by propositions 1 and 2 (they present the material which is conceded), and the Opposition structure is realized by propositions 3 and 4 (the real viewpoint against which the concession is made). The Opposition structure itself consists of a proposition which presents a side of the argument not adhered to by the writer (proposition 3) and a proposition which presents the author's real point of view (proposition 4). Since proposition 4 is the nucleus of the embedded structure which realizes the nucleus of the higher structure, it is the nucleus of the entire passage. Taken together, all the propositions realize the Concession structure.

This passage, being complex, raises the interesting issue of rhetorical *scope*. That is, if propositions 1 and 2 are adjuncts, what are they adjuncts to? Are they adjuncts just to proposition 4 (the main nucleus of the passage), or are they adjuncts to the entire nucleus of their structure, which happens to be realized by an embedded R-structure? The answer is clearly the latter. An adjunct has within its scope its nucleus, even if that nucleus is realized by another R-structure (and even if *that* R-structure is realized by another R-structure, and so on, indefinitely); and of course the reverse is also true: a nucleus has within its scope its adjunct, regardless of the internal structure of that adjunct. Using scoping arguments of this type often helps to understand the relative levels of R-structures, and in turn the hierarchical organization of texts.

(1) What to do?
(2) Simply send for Harry Fujita, 47, the founder of Iwasaki Images of America and the Picasso of fake foods.

(3) Fujita's Torrance, Calif. factory can turn out munchable-looking wax-and-vinyl copies of virtually anything. (*People*, March 19, 1984)

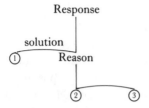

In this passage the highest structure is a Response structure (question–answer), with the adjunct realized by proposition 1 and the nucleus realized by an embedded Reason structure, which is realized by propositions 2 and 3. Note that propositions 2 and 3 are in a response relation to proposition 1, not a reason relation (they are in a reason relation to one another). The nucleus of the embedded Reason structure is proposition 2, and since the Reason structure realizes the nucleus of the higher structure, proposition 2 is the nucleus for the passage.

4.2 Validity in the analyses

In analyzing the texts for this study, it was my goal to construct analyses that approached the rhetorical structures intended by the author of the text in question. This goal is obviously not perfectly attainable, since as readers we bring our own experience, interests, and needs to the process of constructing an interpretation of a text (van Dijk and Kintsch 1983). However, in each case I tried to construct an analysis that was probable (Hirsch 1967: 236):

To establish a reading as probable it is first necessary to show, with reference to the norms of language, that it is possible. This is the criterion of legitimacy: the reading must be permissible within the public norms of the language in which the text was composed. The second criterion is that of correspondence: the reading must account for each linguistic component in the text. Whenever a reading arbitrarily ignores linguistic components or inadequately accounts for them, the reading may be presumed improbable. The third criterion is that of generic appropriateness: if the text follows the conventions of a scientific essay, for example, it is inappropriate to construe the kind of allusive meaning found in casual conversation. When these three preliminary criteria have been satisfied, there remains a fourth criterion which gives significance to all the rest, the criterion of plausibility or *coherence*.

It should thus be clear that the types of analyses offered in the remainder of this study are not random construals of the texts; they are valid attempts at arriving at an appropriate structure for the text.

4.3 Summary

In this chapter I have presented the basic concepts and tools of rhetorical structure analysis. In the next chapter, we will see how these elements are used in the analysis of naturally occurring written English expository texts, and will determine what relationships can be discerned between the structural analyses and the patterns of anaphora exhibited.

5 *Anaphora in expository written English texts*

5.1 Introduction

In this chapter I examine the distribution of pronouns and full noun phrases in some expository written English texts. The structural analysis technique used will be rhetorical structure analysis.

The anaphoric patterns established in this chapter are presented in the two modes discussed in Chapter 3. These two modes, it will be recalled, are the context-determines-use mode and the use-determines-context mode (see also Chapter 3 for a discussion of these modes). I argued in Chapter 3 that both of these modes are always present for conversationally interacting parties, although in any particular instance one may be more strongly felt than the other. The argument for this view runs as follows:

1 Anaphoric form X is the unmarked form for a context like the one the participant is in now.
2 By using anaphoric form X, then, the participant displays an understanding that the context is of that sort.
3 If the participant displays an understanding that the context is of that sort, then the other parties may change their understandings about the nature of the context to be in accord with the understanding displayed (cf. McHoul 1982).

I would like to propose now that this same cycle of factors lies behind anaphora in writing as well. Even though the parties (writer and reader) are not co-present at either the time of writing or the time of reading and hence cannot directly participate in such a fluid display of understandings, each feels the other's presence in a way that strongly influences their behavior towards the text. That is, for a text to be successful (at least in our audience-oriented culture), the writer must *anticipate* the reader's understanding of the text – a developing understanding (since the reader cannot have full access to the writer's plans from the outset) – and must guide the reader to an understanding of the structure of the text which is in accord with the writer's understanding of the text. Similarly, the reader must try to form guesses about the structure of the text as it was intended by the writer, and must therefore be able to form understandings and then abandon them when they seem not to fit. In this indirect way, then, the reader is guided to an interpretation based on what the writer displays, and the writer displays an understanding based on what s/he wants the reader to understand (see the work of literary critic Wolfgang Iser (Iser 1975, for example) for a similar view of the reading process).

It should be kept in mind that, while some of the statements of distribution sound as if they belong in one mode rather than the other, all of the patterns are meant to accommodate the cycle of modes described above.

As in Chapter 3, the structural patterns offered are meant to be the basic patterns, that is, the patterns which will be used when "nothing special" is being done with the reference. The non-structural factors discussed at the end of the chapter, on the other hand, enter into the picture when something besides the signalling of structure is going on. The latter uses of anaphora are treated as "marked," then, because something extra is being done.

5.2   Anaphora in some expository written English texts

5.2.1   The written expository data

The texts used in this study are composed in American English.[1] The instances of written expository texts were selected from four separate sources, in an attempt to have a broad range of expository texts represented. The variety of sources was of course limited by the nature of the phenomenon under study; that is, the text-type had to be a reliable source of multi-paragraph texts containing multiple references to at least one person. In addition, the text-type had to be essentially expository, rather than, say, narrative or procedural. The individual examplars of each source were chosen randomly within these criteria.[2]

The sources ultimately chosen were the following:[3]

1   The *Los Angeles Times*.
2   The *University Bulletin*, the newsletter of the University of California system, which contains information about administrators, faculty, and staff in the UC system.

3 *Bloomsbury: A House of Lions*, a collection of Freudian biographical essays on the members of the Bloomsbury group, written by the literary scholar Leon Edel.

4 *People*, a weekly magazine containing gossip about famous people.

A few miscellaneous examples from other sources were included in the study. These sources included *The Sun* (a San Bernardino county newspaper), *UCItems* (the University of California at Irvine newsletter), the *Santa Monica Seascape* (local newspaper), *Monrovia Today* (local newsletter), and *The Insider* (newsletter for the political group Common Cause).

The selection of texts thus gives a balance of journalistic vs. pseudo-literary, written by professionals vs. amateurs, formal vs. informal, scholarly vs. non-scholarly, informational vs. emotional styles. The texts provide a rich variety of paragraphing styles, text-structuring patterns, length,[4] and subject-matter.

5.2.2 The patterns

The basic pattern for anaphora in my expository texts can be stated as follows:

A pronoun is used to refer to a person if there is a previous mention of that person in a proposition that is active or controlling; otherwise a full NP is used. In other words, by using a pronoun the writer displays to the reader that the intended referent is in an active or controlling proposition, whereas by using a full NP the writer indicates to the reader that the intended referent is outside of these units.[5]

This formulation of the pattern contains two subparts, each of which will be explored in detail below. They can be stated as:

1 A pronoun is used to reference a person mentioned in an active or controlling proposition.

2 All other mentions are done with full NPs.

5.2.3 Pronouns for referents in active or controlling propositions

I have taken the terms *active* and *controlling* from Reichman (1981), and will be using them with essentially their original meaning, though somewhat modified for my own purposes. I will use the term *active* to refer to a proposition in an R-structure (either the adjunct or the nucleus) whose R-structure partner (the nucleus or the adjunct) is being produced. That is, the adjunct of an R-structure is active while its nucleus is being produced; similarly, the nucleus of an R-structure is active while its adjunct is being produced.

A proposition *controlling* while its R-structure partner is *active*. In the following diagram, for example, the nucleus of the Issue structure is controlling while the nucleus of the Conditional structure is active (i.e., its adjunct is being produced):

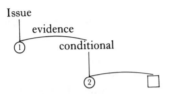

The underlying motivation for these basic patterns is almost certainly reader expectations (or the writer's anticipation of those expectations): the more likely it is that a proposition containing mention of a referent will be elaborated in some way, the more that proposition is treated as a source for pronominal anaphora, hence the more likely it is that the next mention of the referent will be done with a pronoun (cf. Meyer and Rice 1982). For example, if one finds a sentence like the following in a text, one can be almost positive that the next clause will make some mention of the referent:

Elizabeth was a strong ruler:

As the structure gets complex in a direction that suggests no return to the proposition, then the reader may come to assume that the upcoming clauses will not contain mentions of the referent, and hence the referent "falls" from the class of pronominalizable referents.

Reader expectations of this sort are molded by the structure of the text as the reader perceives it, and not by simple measures of distance or prominence. It is for this reason that structure plays such an enormous role in anaphora. But while reader expectations are vague and non-precise notions, text structure can be made more explicit, and hence structure is the natural starting-point for any discussion of anaphora.

The claim made here about the basic pattern of pronominalization in expository written texts is that pronouns are used when their referents are in propositions which are either active or controlling. The first pattern we shall look at is the active pattern.

If there is a mention of a person in the nucleus of an R-structure, then a pronoun can be used in the adjunct of that structure. Examples of this pattern follow. Propositions are numbered for ease of reference.

(1) MacPike will use the second half of her day to complete an administrative fellows program.

(2) *She* will work under vice president Gerald Scherba in the areas of resource allocation and academic personnel. (*The Sun*, July 1983)

The R-structure used in this passage is an Issue structure: the first sentence is the nucleus of the structure and the second sentence is an elaboration adjunct (it provides details for the main claim). There is mention of MacPike in the nucleus of the structure, and in the elaboration adjunct she is referred to with a pronoun. In something more resembling the use-determines-context mode, we could say that the pronoun here creates an interpretation in which the referent is found in an active proposition.

Another example of pronominalization of a referent in an active proposition follows.

(1) Kenneth Vincent Hollywood, who spent his life opening doors for filmdom's rich and famous after flopping big in his own stage debut, has died of cancer.

(2) *He* would have been 61 years old today. (*Los Angeles Times*, August 8, 1983)

The R-structure used in this passage is again an Issue structure: the first sentence is the nucleus (in fact of the whole article) and the second sentence is a background adjunct (information which helps the reader interpret the nucleus). A pronoun is used in the adjunct.

This pattern also includes instances in which the referent is mentioned in the first member of a List structure or a Joint schema – a second mention in the next member of the List or Joint can be done with a pronoun:

(1) She was also the uncompromising woman.

(2)   There could be no deviation from her high personal standards.
(3)   Lady Ottoline Morrell likened her to a Watts painting,
(4)   and *she* discerned melancholy in her face. (*A House of Lions*, p. 77)

The second mention of Lady Ottoline in this passage is a next member of a Joint schema and is done with a pronoun.

The active pattern also holds if the person is mentioned in a pre-posed adjunct of an R-structure and a subsequent mention of that person occurs in the nucleus of the R-structure (this pattern covers approximately 8 per cent of the total number of pronouns in the environment of no interfering referents). The second mention is done with a pronoun. Examples of this type of active pattern follow.

(1)   But as he was approaching 60,
(2)   a chance encounter with humanistic psychologist Dr. Carl Rogers
       made *him* think about a change. (*Los Angeles Times*, July 11, 1983)

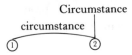

This example manifests a Circumstance R-structure, in which the first clause is the adjunct and the second clause is the nucleus. Notice that the reference in the nucleus is done with a pronoun. Here again, in a more use-determines-context mode, we could say that the pronoun helps to create the active R-structure relation between the first mention and the second mention, inasmuch as it signals to the reader that the referent is to be found in an active (or controlling) proposition.

Another example of this phenomenon follows.

(1)   James Sanford was running in a park in the fall of 1981
(2)   when *he* stepped in a hole. (*Los Angeles Times*, July 19, 1983)

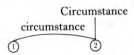

In spite of the subordinator *when* appearing before the second clause, it is the first clause that is the adjunct in this Circumstance structure; the second clause is the nucleus of the structure. We thus have here a mention in an adjunct followed by a mention in the nucleus, done with a pronoun.

I have demonstrated here that a referent mentioned in the adjunct of a simple R-structure can be pronominalized in the nucleus of that R-structure. The simple *active* pattern thus appears to be well-motivated and fully documentable (covering approximately 63 per cent of the pronouns in the environment of no interfering referents).

It should be noted here that the use of pronouns discussed above could also have been predicted by theories of distance, in that there tends in these cases to be a short distance (one or two clauses) between the pronoun and its most recent antecedent mention. We will see later, however, that while theories of distance in anaphora seem to account for a large number of the pronouns used, *overall* they cannot handle the range of anaphoric patterns exhibited by expository texts.

The second pattern of pronominalization in the expository texts I examined is the controlling pattern: in this case, a pronoun is used to refer to a person mentioned in a proposition that is controlling. Recall that a proposition is controlling if its R-structure partner is active.

For our purposes here, I will say that a proposition is active only while the first member of the embedded R-structure is being produced (rather than during the entire embedded structure); thus, when the embedded partner is being produced, the previously active proposition becomes controlling. This pattern does not distinguish between the following two patterns, one in which the second-level adjunct is a terminal node, the other in which it is the source of a further embedded structure.

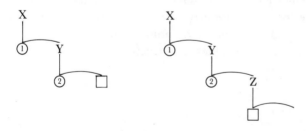

Embeddings with the appropriate pattern of references are fairly rare in my texts, probably because many of the texts are short, and possibly because the types of people-oriented text I have chosen to look at in this study display a flatter structure than other types of text. The one example I have found comes from a longer, non-journalistic text.

(1) Leonard saw these as a "series of psychological curtains which one interposed between oneself and the outside world of 'other people.'"

(2)   It was all part of the process of growing up and also a means of self-concealment and self-defense.

(3)   Particularly valuable in this process was *his* learning of a peculiar ecstasy which comes from "*feeling* the mind work smoothly and imaginatively upon difficult and complicated problems." (*A House of Lions*, p. 25)

The structure of this passage follows.

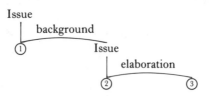

We have a nucleus, *Leonard saw these* . . ., which is *active* while the nucleus of the embedded realization for the adjunct is being constructed (*It was all a part* . . .). When the adjunct of this embedded nucleus is being constructed, the first nucleus becomes controlling. Notice that the reference in the embedded adjunct is done with a pronoun, thus supporting our claim that referents in controlling propositions can be pronominalized.

The controlling pattern also extends to cases in which a referent is mentioned in a nucleus, with its adjunct realized by an embedded structure, and the embedded adjunct is done first (with no mention of the referent). If the subsequent embedded nucleus contains a mention of the referent, then a pronoun can be used to perform the reference. Here again we have an instance of a referent in a controlling proposition being the source of a pronominal reference. An example of the structure for this situation is given below.

(1)   He prospered.

(2)   When Victoria came to the throne

(3)   he was living in a comfortable house in or near Tavistock Square. (*A House of Lions*, p. 19)

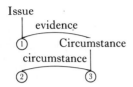

We find in this passage a claim with an evidence adjunct. The evidence adjunct itself contains an adjunct and a nucleus, and the adjunct comes before the nucleus. In this case the Issue nucleus is active while the Circumstance adjunct is produced, becoming controlling when the Circumstance nucleus is being constructed. A pronoun is used for the reference in the Circumstance nucleus.

This pattern differs from the preceding one in the rhetorical status of the "intervening" material; in one case it is the nucleus of an R-structure, and in the other it is an adjunct of an R-structure. This difference is almost sure to have an impact on anaphora, since an adjunct is produced "on behalf" of its nucleus (and hence does not necessarily introduce the next frame for discussion), while the nucleus is the core of the structure. The adjunct thus could be treated as less of an "intrusion" for the purposes of anaphora than the nucleus of an embedded structure. As we shall see somewhat later, this difference between adjunct and nucleus does have an influence on some patterns of anaphora.

Pronominalization is also possible if the *nucleus* is realized by an embedded structure. In the following passage, for example, a referent is mentioned in the nucleus of the embedded structure (i.e. the nucleus of a Circumstance structure), and a subsequent mention of the referent in the adjunct of the higher structure (i.e. the adjunct of an Issue structure) is done with a pronoun.

(1)   MacPike joined the Cal State faculty in 1978 as a lecturer
(2)   after teaching three years at the University of Hawaii.
(3)   *She* received an appointment as an associate professor in 1981. (*The Sun*, July 1983)

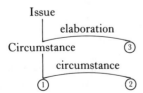

The embedded nucleus (*MacPike joined* . . .) contains a mention of the referent. The higher adjunct (*She received an appointment* . . .) also contains a mention of the referent; this second reference is done with a pronoun.

The controlling pattern is fairly minor in the texts I examined, covering only approximately 2 per cent of the pronouns in the environment of no interfering referents.

In the preceding discussion we have seen that a proposition is treated as controlling if a physically contiguous R-structure is being developed; now we will see that a physically distant R-structure can "tie" back to an earlier proposition and thereby make that proposition controlling. This pattern of tying to a proposition other than the immediately preceding one is called a *return pop*, because the writer is returning to an earlier, superordinate, node.[6] In my texts, a pattern that is seen frequently is nucleus – adjunct – adjunct, where the second adjunct is an adjunct for the nucleus rather than for the preceding adjunct. A diagram of this type of structure is presented below, where the adjuncts are numbered in their order of occurrence.

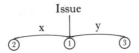

A return pop can also occur if a list of items is being enumerated and there is a side adjunct on one of the list members, followed by a return to the List structure:

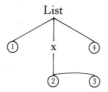

As we would expect from the formulation of the basic pattern above, propositions which are put into a controlling state by virtue of a return pop can be the sources of pronominalization. The use of pronouns in return pops is quite a delicate matter, however, in that any complication of structure appears to prevent their appearance in this situation. That is, whether a return is done with a pronoun or not depends heavily on the intervening "popped-over" material.

The first pattern of return pop that I have identified can be stated as follows: a pronoun is used in a return pop if the "popped-over" material contains mentions of the pronoun's referent. In this case the degree of structural complexity of the popped-over material can be considered for now[7] somewhat irrelevant. Examples of returns done with pronouns in the case of same-referent mentions in the popped-over material are given below.

(1) Bob "Smitty" Smith will be installed as the 1984 president of the Monrovia Chamber of Commerce at the annual January dinner.

(2) He has been a partner in the Monrovia Travel Agency with Bob Bennett since 1974,

(3) but after the first year, when Bennett retires, Smith will become the sole owner.

(4) An 11-year member of the Chamber, Smith serves on the Ambassadors committee, a group which systematically visits the over 600 members of the Chamber in a series of two- or three-day "blitzes."

(5) He has served on the Chamber's Board of Directors for three years,

(6) and he is a member of the public relations committee.

(7) *His* most recent community involvement has been appointment to the Centennial Committee. . . . (*Monrovia Today*, January 1984)

For now we will consider only the italicized reference (*His*) in this passage. The structure for the whole text is given below (the position in the diagram of an adjunct to the right or to the left of a nucleus is unimportant and usually reflects limitations on space).

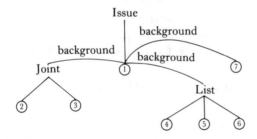

The nucleus of the passage is the first sentence – that is, the fact of Smith's installment is the "news" which the article is meant to convey. The next sentence, represented by a Joint structure, is a background structure on the nucleus of the passage. The next three propositions (in a List structure) are another background structure on the main nucleus (hence a return pop, but not the one we are concerned with now). The proposition containing the italicized pronoun is a third background adjunct off of the main nucleus, and is the return pop we want to examine now. In this text we thus have a nucleus and three adjuncts on that nucleus, each produced after the other. Notice that the second and third adjuncts are not adjuncts of the first adjunct, but tie directly to the nucleus. This is what makes them return pops.

The third adjunct (the second return pop) contains a reference to Smith that is done with a pronoun. It is my contention here that the reason for this pronoun return pop is the fact that the two preceding adjuncts, as well as the nucleus, contain multiple references to Smith. The pronoun in the third adjunct thus correlates with the appearance of references in the first and second adjuncts.

Although from a use-determines-context point of view it would be tempting to say that the pronoun in this case *accomplishes* the return pop, I do not think that such a strong statement is warranted by the data. There are two reasons for this belief. First, we saw many examples earlier in which pronouns were used in contexts other than return pops; second, we will see later on that return pops are often done with full NPs. Pronouns are thus neither necessary nor sufficient for the achievement of a return pop.

Another example of a pronoun used in the context of a return pop is given below.

(1)   Jo Anne Brannen, a six-year employee of Security Pacific Bank, was presented with the Chamber of Commerce courtesy award by Betty Sandford, chairman of the public relations committee.

(2)   Nominees are suggested by residents or customers.

(3)   Mrs. Brannen started as a part-time teller

(4)   and now serves as the branch auditor.

(5)   If she has a secret to getting along with people,

(6)   she believes it is that she has worked with the public all of her life,

(7)   and really enjoys people.

(8)   *She* has two children, ages 19 and 17, and five stepchildren, all grown. (*Monrovia Today*, January 1984).

The structure of this passage follows.

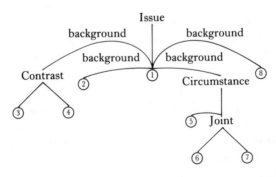

The first sentence represents the nucleus of the passage – Brannen's receiving the award is the news of this little article. The second sentence (and second paragraph) is a background structure off of the nucleus. The third paragraph is a further background structure off of the nucleus, and the final sentence given is a third background structure. This passage thus has the basic structure of the preceding passage: a nucleus and three background adjuncts. The second and third adjuncts are return pops. The last pop is done with a pronoun.

Again, it is my argument here that a pronoun is used for this particular return pop because the immediately preceding adjunct, which has been popped over (as well as the nucleus), contains mentions of the relevant person. It is this intervening mentioning of the referent that allows the use of a pronoun in the return.

This first pattern of pronominalization in return pops is the second most common pattern for pronominalization, covering roughly 23 per cent of the pronouns counted in the environment of no interfering referents.

The second pattern of pronominalization in return pops can be described as follows: pronouns can be used in return pops where there is no mention of the referent in the popped-over adjunct, if very special circumstances hold. In essence, the popped-over material must be extremely limited in structure: it must not contain a new Issue structure or any other structure with its own complex nucleus–adjunct structure. The most common type of intervening material in this case is a single node – for example, a terminal background node, or a terminal elaboration node – although in a few instances I found intervening material which contained a few equal-status terminal nodes (as in a List structure or a Joint structure). Anything of greater internal complexity "induces" a full NP in the return pop. This second pattern of pronominalization in return pops is fairly rare, accounting for only about 3 per cent of the pronouns in the environment of no interfering referents.

My guess about this restriction on anaphora is that when a complex adjunct is being developed, the reader may begin to assume that the nucleus is not going to be returned to, and hence the nucleus loses its potential status of *active* for the reader.[8] That is, the nucleus becomes, in a sense, closed off for the reader, so that a return must be done with a full NP. If, on the other hand, the adjunct is clearly limited in complexity, then there may be fairly high expectations that the writer will return to the nucleus, and therefore the referent in the nucleus remains pronominalizable. The nucleus in this case retains its potential *active* status even while other propositions are being constructed. Here again we see that reader expectations (and writers' anticipation of those expectations) form the mold for patterns of anaphora.

Examples of pronouns in return pops with no mentions of the referent in the popped-over adjunct are given below.

(1)   As important in Leonard's rearing as the Old Testament sense of virtue and goodness were large chunks of diluted Baptist doctrine imparted by his favorite nurse some years earlier.

(2)   The nurse was a Somersetshire woman, with straight-parted black hair and a smooth, oval farm-girl face.

(3)   She read to *him* in the nursery at Lexham Gardens. . . . (*A House of Lions*, p. 22)

The structure of this passage is something like the following:

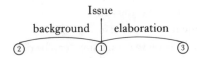

The nucleus of this chunk of text is the first sentence. The second sentence is a background adjunct off of the nucleus, and the third sentence is an elaboration off of the nucleus. The third sentence is thus a return pop which pops over the second sentence. The first adjunct (second sentence) contains no mentions of Leonard, and yet the return pop can be done with a pronoun[9] because the structure of the first adjunct is so simple – a terminal background node.

(1)   Like most hedonists, he preferred to look neither backward nor forward.

(2)   The here and now, the picture in front of him, the woman he was with, the bird in flight – this was life:

(3)   the rest was history.

(4)   The future could assuredly take care of itself.

(5)   *He* found himself at one with Proust in the thought that "the only certainty in life is change." (*A House of Lions*, p. 28)

The nucleus of this passage is the first sentence, which contains a reference to Clive Bell. From *The here and now* to *the future could* . . . we have an elaboration adjunct with three equal parts (a Contrast structure: now vs. past vs. future). The last sentence is a second adjunct on the nucleus, thus a return pop. This return pop can be done with a pronoun because of the relatively simple structure of the intervening adjunct; although it has some internal structure, it does not begin something new (as would a new Issue structure) and it does not have a complex nucleus–adjunct structure.

The structure of the passage follows.

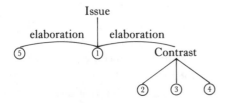

With this pattern of return pop we are stretching the limits of distance-based theories of anaphora. Notice that in some of the passages above there are gaps of two or three clauses between the pronoun and the most recent mention of the referent. The traditional theory could still predict pronouns under these conditions, but critically could not distinguish these cases, in which three clauses do not induce the use of full NP, from cases in which three clauses could – for *structural* reasons – cause the writer to use a full NP. Thus, while distance theories could predict the uses of pronominalization I have presented so far, they could not *selectively* predict these cases, as a structure-based theory can. For example, Givón and his colleagues (Givón 1983) in fact predict more pronominalization than is actually displayed by the expository texts I examined for this study.

I suggested earlier that if a List structure were being created and there was an adjunct off of one of the members of the list, then a return to the List structure is done with a pronoun. This pattern holds only if the adjunct is structurally simple (like the adjuncts in the examples above). Examples of this pattern are given below.

(1) His re-entry into Hollywood came with the movie "Brainstorm,"
(2) but its completion and release has been delayed by the death of co-star Natalie Wood.
(3) *He* plays Hugh Hefner of Playboy magazine in Bob Fosse's "Star 80."
(4) It's about Dorothy Stratton, the Playboy Playmate who was killed by her husband.
(5) *He* also stars in the movie "Class." (*Los Angeles Times*, July 18, 1983)

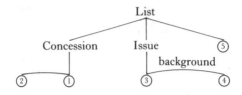

In this passage we get a list of the movies Robertson starred in after his temporary exile from Hollywood. Thus, even though the first member of the list has an adjunct which does not mention Robertson (*but its completion* . . .), the next member of the list can contain a pronoun. This pattern is repeated between the second and third members of the list: the second member has a background structure off of it that does not mention Robertson (*It's about Dorothy Stratton* . . .), but the third member starts right up with a pronoun. Notice that in a strictly linear view of this text we might think that *he* could be ambiguous in the last sentence, since there is another male referent in the immediately preceding clause (the husband). The hierarchical approach, which sees the text as a *List* structure, makes a more accurate prediction about pronominalization.

The patterns examined in this section describe the major uses of pronouns in return pops. In the next section we shall see how full NPs tend to be used in returns.

5.2.4   Full NPs elsewhere

When the structural relation between two mentions of a referent (or the propositions containing those mentions) is one other than the relations we have seen above – that is, other than active, controlling, and certain types of return pops – full NPs are used.

Passages illustrating the use of full NP in relations other than active and controlling are given below.

Clive looked and thought about pictures through his ambivalence of conformity and rebellion, often tinged also with unconscious pomposity in his endeavor to be "serious" – seeing what the painter had done in his own effort (like Clive's) to make something out of the world, to give life some shape other than the patterned shapes of convention. He had, said Virginia Woolf, an odd gift for making one talk sense. All Clive's life was a quest for a superior "civilization." Clive needed answers to questions that occurred neither to Leonard nor Lytton, nor to the Stephen girls, since they had been bred from the first to possess the answers.

Much of this seems to have been latent in the boy, who in a good-natured way accepted and rebelled against his mother's religious precepts and his father's concrete world. And yet he wanted approval. He wanted to be right, gentlemanly, proper; the improprieties would come later. *Virginia*, in her continuing remarks about him, said he had the mind of "a peculiarly prosaic and literal type". . . . (*A House of Lions*, p. 31)

In this passage, the first mention of Virginia Woolf is part of a proposition that provides support for a claim about Clive. In the following sentence we have another claim about Clive, which thus pops over the proposition containing reference to Woolf. As we saw in Chapter 3, a return pop closes off the material over which it has popped; thus, after the pop back to claims about Clive, the material in which Woolf is mentioned is closed, and hence certainly not active or controlling. The next mention of her, again in an evidencing proposition, is done with a full NP, as we would have expected.

Return pops are also done with full NPs if the constraining criteria described above for pronominalization in return pops are not met. That is, if there are no mentions of the relevant referent in the popped-over material, and/or the popped-over material is structurally complex, then the return pop will contain a full NP reference. Examples illustrating this pattern are given below.

(1)   He spoke, as all his friends have testified, with two voices.
(2)   One was deep and manly;
(3)   the other was tiny and a squeak.
(4)   One had warm baritone notes filled with emotion;
(5)   the other was somehow the piping voice of childhood, perhaps learned from a bevy of sisters who filled the Strachey home.
(6)   It has been said that the entire Strachey family possessed this kind of squeak.
(7)   Leonard Woolf remarked that after being with a Strachey one somehow went away squeaking a little inside.
(8)   However that may be, the two voices of *Lytton Strachey* were the voices of the masculinity to which he generally aspired – but without real struggle – and the femininity that was his by virtue of his rearing and environment. . . . (*A House of Lions*, p. 34)

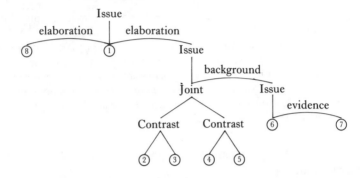

In this passage, the complexity of the structure starting with *one was deep*
and going to *went away squeaking a little inside* contra-indicates the use of a
pronoun in the return pop (the proposition containing the italicized full
NP).

Another example of full NP used in a return pop which pops over
structurally complex material follows.

Leonard was a young Spartan in the heart of chaotic London. Behind him were
centuries of persecution, violence, death. No more, I suppose, than the centuries
behind the Irish or the Huguenots – or the Puritans, before these also became
persecutors. Yet with important differences. Leonard's people had a longer history
of dispersal, an ingrained learned toughness, a curious mixture of inferiorities and
stubbornness, pride and consciousness of race and status. They had seemed at first
"outlandish" in England; this was a grave handicap in a society with strong
boundaries, cultivated stratifications. Leonard Woolf's heritage was strong: a
Biblical ethic, a sense of the importance of work, a built-in discipline of strength, of
control. One had to be proof against life insults. For the centuries had piled insults
on the Jews and made them prize tenaciously a heritage of righteousness that is the
world order imposed on chaos by the Old Testament – which itself is a record of
chaos, crime, rapacity, persecution and privilege.
    Leonard Woolf combined Old Testament virtues with an ingrained English sense
of "fair play". . . . (*A House of Lions*, p. 21)

Although it is not altogether clear to which nucleus the last line ties back
(probably either *Leonard was a young Spartan* or *Leonard Woolf's heritage
was strong*), it is clear that in any case the material popped-over is
structurally complex, as we have defined that notion here.

We have seen in this discussion that the basic pattern is to use full NPs
when the proposition containing the relevant last mention of a referent is not
in an active or controlling state, or if the criteria for pronominalization in
return pops are not met. Below I present a discussion of full NPs in yet

another structural context: that of indicating breaks in the rhetorical structure of the text.

5.3   Rhetorical structure breaks and anaphora

We saw in earlier sections that pronouns commonly occur in the following environments:

1   In the nucleus or adjunct of an R-structure, if the relevant referent is mentioned in the R-structure partner.
2   In a return pop adjunct, if the adjunct "popped over" (*a*) contains mentions of the relevant referent, or (*b*) is structurally non-complex.

It is clear when one examines expository texts, however, that pronouns are not used on every occasion in which they are structurally warranted; full NPs are rampant in such texts. What, then, determines when full NPs will be used when pronouns would have been structurally possible?

The proposal I would like to offer here suggests that it is another type of structural property that "induces" the use of full NP in these cases.[10] The structural property at work is one of demarcating new rhetorical units.[11]

Consider the following short text and its rhetorical structure diagram. Propositions are numbered to ease the task of following the schema.

(1)   James S. Albertson has been appointed acting academic vice president by the Regents following President Saxon's recommendation.

(2)   The appointment is effective from March 1 until a permanent academic vice president is named.

(3)   Academic Vice President Donald C. Swain earlier was named president of the University of Louisville.

(4)   *Albertson* will be responsible for academic planning and program review, student affairs, financial aid, admissions, student loan collections, student affirmative action, basic skills, the Education Abroad Program, library plans and policies and UC Press.

(5)   *He* also is responsible for UC Extension, summer sessions, instructional media, Continuing Education of the Bar, and liaison with the Academic Senate, the Student Body Presidents' Council and the California Postsecondary Education Commission.

(6)   *Albertson* has been special assistant to Swain since 1978.

(7)   For four years prior to that *he* was assistant academic vice president.

(8)   *He* joined UC in 1973 as director of analytical studies.

(9)   *Albertson* is a graduate in classics at St. Louis University.

(10) *He* earned his M.A. in philosophy there in 1953

(11) and received the Ph.D. in physics in 1958 at Harvard.

(12) *He* joined the faculty at Loyola University of Los Angeles in 1962

(13) and became chairman of the department before *he* left in 1968 to join
       the faculty of the University of Santa Clara as professor of physics.

(14) *He* was also academic vice president at Santa Clara. (*University
       Bulletin*, March 23, 1981)

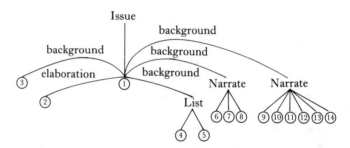

I claimed in Chapter 4 that the Issue structure is the dominating (i.e.
topmost) structure in most texts, as it is in this short article. I would like to
propose now that each of the adjuncts of an Issue structure holds the
possibility of being a new rhetorical unit, and that each of these new units
tends to be associated with a full NP, even though by other structural
criteria a pronoun would have been appropriate. Notice that all the
adjunct-initial propositions (propositions 4, 6, and 9) which could have had
a pronoun[12] in fact contain full NPs, while the propositions which do not
begin a new Issue adjunct (propositions 5, 7, 8, 10, 12, 13, and 14 – these
continue either List structures or Narrative structures) are done with
pronouns. That is, full NPs (at least in the texts I examined for this study)
appear to be associated with the beginnings of Issue adjuncts, even though
pronouns can also be used in those slots (Clancy 1980; Tomlin,
forthcoming; and Marslen-Wilson *et al.* 1982 discuss a similar relationship
in narratives between episode-initial slot and use of full NP).[13]

This type of pattern strongly represents the use-determines-context
mode: by using a full NP at a particular point in a text, especially if the
referent's identity is easily retrievable from the immediately preceding
material, the writer *creates* the effect of beginning a new rhetorical unit. It
is thus not merely the case that the context of a new unit induces a writer to
use a full NP; the writer actively creates that new unit through the use of the
anaphoric form.

Notice, with this association of new rhetorical unit and full NP, that it would not be accurate to say that pronouns are used when the referent is mentioned in the immediately preceding text, and that full NPs are used when the referent is mentioned further back in the text. In my expository texts, fully 38 per cent (204/541) of the full NPs had their referents mentioned in the immediately preceding clause, so it is not simple distance that triggers the use of one anaphoric device over the other. Rather, it is the rhetorical organization of that distance that determines whether a pronoun or a full NP is appropriate. Here we find a clear instance in which the non-selective formulations predicting pronominalization whenever the referential distance is small simply fail to account for a widespread anaphoric phenomenon.

It should be kept in mind that the pattern in this section is, in a sense, hierarchically superordinate to the other basic patterns and would, in a rule-ordered system, have to be ordered before the basic patterns in order to ensure correct output.

Table 5.1 supports the claim that new rhetorical units are associated with the use of a full NP. Twenty short expository articles were used as the basis for the figures. Of all of the new rhetorical units started, 65 per cent (77/118) contained full NPs, while of the continuing rhetorical units, 10 per cent (6/59) contained full NPs. Thus, while pronouns and full NPs can appear in either type of slot, there is a skewing of full NP towards new rhetorical unit, and of pronoun towards continuing rhetorical unit.

Although rhetorical breaks are often signalled in expository prose by paragraph breaks, it would not be accurate to say simply that in expository prose all paragraphs begin with full NPs. One of the propositions containing a pronoun in the passage above is paragraph-initial, though not rhetorical unit-initial. Thus, while paragraphs are rhetorical units of a sort, they are not the major units which influence anaphora; the units which do influence anaphora are R-structures, most notably the adjuncts off of Issue structures.

Table 5.1 *Anaphoric device and position in rhetorical unit*

	New rhetorical unit	Same rhetorical unit	Total
Full NP	77 (93%) (65%)	6 (7%) (10%)	83
Pronoun	41 (44%) (35%)	53 (56%) (90%)	94
Total	118	59	177

There seem to be, then, two conflicting structural principles at work in determining anaphora in the expository texts I have looked at: the first says that under certain specifiable conditions a pronoun is appropriate; and the second says that if certain other conditions also hold, a *full NP* can be appropriate. The result is that neither principle is followed 100 per cent of the time, but rather each text is some sort of compromise between them.[14]

Further examples of the association between full NP and unit-initial slot are given below.

(1)   Theodore L. Hullar has been appointed executive vice chancellor at Riverside, succeeding Carlton R. Bovell.

(2)   Bovell announced his resignation to return to full-time duties as a biology professor and researcher on campus.

(3)   *Hullar* is director of the Agricultural Experiment Station and director for research at Cornell University.

(4)   At Cornell, *Hullar* established three important programs – the Cornell Biotechnology Institute and New York State Center for Biotechnology, the Institute for Comparative and Environmental Toxicology, and the Ecosystems Research Center.

(5)   As executive vice chancellor, *Hullar* is responsible for the administration of faculty and academic policy, involving all colleges, professional schools and departments.

(6)   In addition, *he* will oversee the Graduate Division and Research, the library, registrar and admissions, student recruitment, affirmative action, University Extension and Summer Session.

(7)   In the chancellor's absence, *Hullar* will act as chief executive for the campus.

(8)   Chancellor Tomas Rivera said "Dr. Hullar . . ." (*University Bulletin*, January 16–20, 1984)

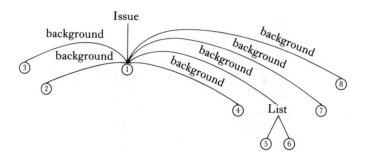

All the new adjuncts are started with full NPs; the one proposition which does not start a new adjunct but continues List structure (6) is done with a pronoun (*In addition, he will oversee . . .*).

There is thus a correlation between non-new units and pronouns, as well as between new units and full NPs.

Further examples of members of a List structure being referred to with a pronoun are given below.

(1) Lytton's speech was filled with the rhetoric of the past.
(2) *He* knew his Rousseau;
(3) *he* knew his Voltaire;
(4) *he* even knew his President de Brosses! (*A House of Lions*, p. 39)

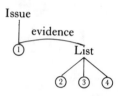

(1) We see many Vanessas in the portraits that remain of her, especially those painted by Duncan Grant.
(2) The young face was smooth, with firmly lined brows and liquid gray-green eyes.
(3) *She* had sensuous lips.
(4) *She* rarely used makeup.
(5) Somewhere Virginia speaks of "her passionate mouth."
(6) *Her* voice was beautifully modulated;
(7) *her* words were carefully paced. (*A House of Lions*, p. 78)

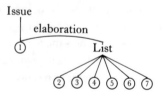

(1) Hunter does what he can to keep elocution alive.
(2) *He* spoke continuously for three hours from a platform in Memorial Park during Claremont's 1979 Fourth of July festivities.
(3) The next year, at the same rostrum, *he* stretched it out four hours.
(4) The next Fourth of July, on a similar platform half a continent away, *he* talked nearly six hours. (*Los Angeles Times*, July 3, 1983)

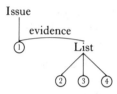

(1)   Against such formidable appeal, his opponents no doubt were readying grenades,

(2)   but up to Super Tuesday they could throw only marshmallows:

(3)   For nearly 17 years *he* had shaved a year off his actual age . . . ;

(4)   in 1961 *he* had officially shortened his name from Hartpence . . . ;

(5)   at 43, *he* had obtained an appointment to the Naval Reserve. (*People*, March 26, 1984)

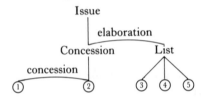

In each of these examples, the references within the List structures which are coreferential with the referent in the nucleus (off of which the List is an adjunct) are done with pronouns. This distribution supports the hypothesis that it is *new* rhetorical units that are started with full NPs. In cases where no new unit is started, a pronoun is used.

The following passage brings up another principle in choosing a full NP over a pronoun: the greater the *internal structure* of the just-created structure, the more likely we are to find the current proposition done with a full NP, even if the current proposition is a next member in a List or Narrative structure. That is, a return to a List structure is more likely to be done with a full NP if the preceding member of the List has its own adjunct (that is, a structure of its own) than if the preceding member has no internal structure.

Compare the List and Narrative structures of the Albertson article (above) with the List structure in the Glaser article (below): the non-initial members of those structures in the Albertson text are done with pronouns, while the non-initial member of the List in the Glaser text is done with a full NP (proposition 6). The reason for this difference in anaphora, according to the hypothesis proposed here, is that the members of the List and Narrative structures in the Albertson article have no internal structure – they are all terminal nodes; the first member of the List in question in the Glaser text, however, has a background adjunct (giving the names of the laboratories), and the next member of the List (*Glaser will also assist* . . .) is done with a full NP.

Remember that in an earlier section we saw that a return to a List structure over an adjunct of a preceding member of the List could be done with a pronoun (for example in the Robertson passage above), so I am not claiming here that such a move *must* be done with a full NP; rather, given this other set of structuring principles which takes into account the internal articulation (Koffka 1935) of the preceding and current units, it *can* be done with a full NP.

(1) A new position at the University has been filled, involving responsibility for matters concerning the four Laboratories that UC manages for the US Department of Energy.

(2) Harold Glaser, a consultant to the US Office of Management and Budget, will serve in the new position as a special assistant to President Saxon.

(3) The appointment is another step taken by UC to strengthen its oversight of the DOE Laboratories.

(4) *Glaser* will assist Saxon and Vice President William B. Fretter in fulfilling their oversight responsibility for the four Laboratories.

(5) They are the Laboratory of Biomedical and Environmental Science at Los Angeles, the Lawrence Berkeley Laboratory, the Lawrence Livermore National Laboratory and the Los Alamos National Scientific Laboratory in New Mexico.

(6) *Glaser* will also assist the Regent's Committee on Oversight of the DOE Laboratories and two committees that are advisory to Saxon on laboratory matters. (The two committees are the Scientific and Academic Advisory Committee established in 1971 and the recently authorized Committee on Health, Safety and Environment.)

(7) *Glaser's* responsibilities will include preparation of background papers, handling requests for special studies, drafting reports, developing agendas for meetings of the various committees and preparing background materials for the meetings.

(8) Until recently *Glaser* had been director of NASA's Solar Terrestrial Division, responsible for planning, implementing and managing most of the US effort in solar terrestrial research.

(9)   Earlier *he* had been in charge of solar physics at NASA.

(10)   *He* has also worked at NSF and the National Bureau of Standards,

(11)   and *he* was detailed to the White House staff in 1971 and 1972.

(12)   *Glaser* also worked in the Office of Naval Research, at the Naval Research Laboratory, and at the Applied Physics Laboratory of Johns Hopkins University.

(13)   (The UC Regents voted at their June meeting to renew for five years their contracts with the US Department of Energy to manage the four DOE Labs. The vote was 11–4.) (*University Bulletin*, July 13, 1981)

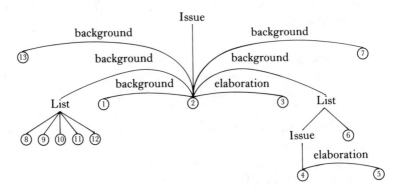

In the preceding discussion we have seen that full NPs can, and very often do, occur in structural environments in which pronouns would have been predicted to occur. I claimed that the motivation for the use of full NPs in these situations is *rhetorical organization*, whereby the internal cohesiveness and the external discohesiveness of rhetorical units is displayed to the reader. Notions of participant continuity and paragraphing were shown to be ineffective in accounting for the rich patterning of anaphora in these texts.

5.4   Anaphora in the environment of different-gender referents

In this section I examine the effect on anaphoric patterning of the appearance of different-gender referents.

The pattern for anaphora in the environment of different-gender referents is somewhat more restricted than the basic pattern described in section 5.2. It can be stated in essence as:

A pronoun is used to refer to a person in a different-gender environment if there is a previous mention of that person in a proposition which is active; otherwise a full NP is used.

As this pattern is stated, then, pronominalization is limited to the active pattern, which includes R-structure partners and return pops.

5.4.1 Pronominalization in the active pattern

As we saw above, a proposition is active if its R-structure partner is being produced. In the following passages, we have examples of two different-gender referents in the same proposition, and one or both of them are pronominalized in the R-structure partner:

(1) This time he married a sturdy Scotswoman with all the hardihood and endurance of the north – and of her race.

(2) Year after year *she* bore *him* children. (*A House of Lions*, p. 35)

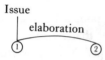

Here, both people mentioned in the nucleus of the R-structure are referred to with pronouns in the R-structure partner (the adjunct).

A similar example follows, in which two referents, of different genders, appear in the nucleus of the R-structure, and both are pronominalized in the adjunct.

(1) At three Vanessa had a baby brother aged one and a half.

(2) *She* mothered *him*. (*A House of Lions*, p. 79)

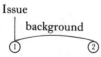

If the nucleus is realized by an embedded R-structure, and one of the referents is mentioned in the nucleus of that embedded structure and the other, different-gender, referent is mentioned in the adjunct of the embedded structure, then either person can be referred to using a pronoun in the higher adjunct. An example of this pattern follows.

(1) "The most ridiculous boy," said Lady Strachey

(2)   when Lytton reached the age of speech,
(3)   for *he* spoke his fantasies aloud. (*A House of Lions*, p. 35)

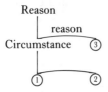

In this passage, the higher nucleus is realized by an embedded Circumstance structure: the female referent appears in the nucleus of this embedded structure and the male referent appears in the adjunct of the embedded structure. Notice that the reference to the male person in the higher adjunct is done with a pronoun. The active pattern covers approximately 46 per cent of the pronouns in the environment of different-gender referents.

When a proposition is returned to via a return pop, it becomes active again. And, in fact, we saw earlier in this chapter that return pops to a nucleus are done with pronouns if the adjunct "popped over" is structurally simple. Below I will demonstrate that, following this pattern, a return pop is done with a pronoun even if the popped-over adjunct mentions a different-gender referent, if and only if that adjunct is structurally simple. Examples follow.

(1)   His re-entry into Hollywood came with the movie "Brainstorm,"
(2)   but its completion and release has been delayed by the death of co-star Natalie Wood.
(3)   *He* plays Hugh Hefner of Playboy magazine in Bob Fosse's "Star 80. "
(4)   It's about Dorothy Stratton, the Playboy Playmate who was killed by her husband.
(5)   *He* also stars in the movie "Class." (*Los Angeles Times*, July 18, 1983)

The structure of this passage can be represented as:

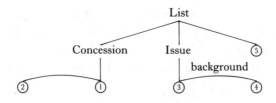

In each instance in which I have italicized the pronoun (propositions 3 and 5), we have a return pop to a list structure over a non-complex adjunct containing a reference to a different-gender person.

Another example follows.

(1) Alexis C. Jackson has been appointed assistant vice president for business management at the University.
(2) The appointment, recommended by President Saxon, was approved by the Regents at their March meeting.
(3) The appointment was to be effective April 1 or as soon thereafter as *she* has been able to relocate to California. (*University Bulletin*, April 20, 1981)

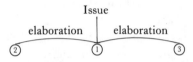

In this passage, we have a nucleus (*Alexis . . . has been appointed . . .*), then an elaboration adjunct with a male referent mentioned in it, and then a return pop over the adjunct to create a second elaboration adjunct. The return is done with a pronoun, even though a different-gender referent is present in the popped-over adjunct. The return pop pattern accounts for roughly 50 per cent of the pronouns in the environment of different-gender referents.

In all of my texts I found one passage in which pronominalization was possible in a different-gender environment when the relevant proposition was controlling rather than active. This passage is given below.

(1) He prospered.
(2) When Victoria came to the throne,
(3) *he* was living in a comfortable house. (*A House of Lions*, p. 19)

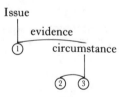

It is worth noting about this passage that the "interfering" different-gender referent comes in the adjunct, rather than the nucleus, of the embedded structure, and in addition the adjunct itself is structurally simple (a terminal node). Both of these factors no doubt work together to allow pronominalization in a situation other than the active pattern established above.

5.4.2   Full NPs elsewhere

Full NPs are used in cases where anything more "distant" than the active pattern is in progress, and in return pops if the popped-over material is structurally complex.

Passages illustrating the use of full NP in a pattern other than the active pattern are presented below.

(1)   Leonard got from her both the pleasures and fear of public events, "the horrors and iniquities of the great world of society and politics as recorded in the *Baptist Times*, about the year 1885."

(2)   And all this in the untroubled atmosphere of the Lexham Gardens third-floor nursery, where the boy felt snug and safe.

(3)   The fire blazed behind the tall guard;

(4)   the kettle sang musically,

(5)   and the music mingled with *the nurse*'s reading of serious things. (*A House of Lions*, p. 22)

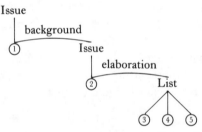

The higher nucleus mentions both the referents – Leonard and his nurse. We then have an adjunct/nucleus which mentions only Leonard, and the adjunct on this last item – a List structure – contains a reference to the nurse, done with a full NP. We thus have a controlling pattern, and a full NP is used for the critical reference.

Another example follows.

(1)   Still later she had John Singer Sargeant as her master;

(2)   like Furse, he had studied in France.

(3)   He was a sympathetic and encouraging teacher, a large imposing presence.

(4)   *Vanessa* liked his voice. (*A House of Lions*, p. 83)

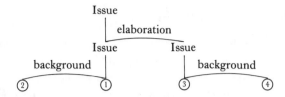

Here again we have a controlling pattern, with a different-gender referent in the embedded nucleus, and a full NP used for the reference in the embedded adjunct.

It was claimed in section 5.2.3 that return pops over structurally complex material are associated with the use of full NP, even if no other referents are involved. The presence of different-gender referents does not alter the pattern: it is followed if the popped-over material contains mentions of a different-gender referent as well. However, since the pattern is basically the same as the one illustrated in section 5.2.3, I will not discuss it further here.

In this section we have seen, again, that it is not just distance or the introduction of another referent that determines the anaphoric device chosen; rather, it is the structural organization of that distance, and of that other mention, that determines anaphoric patterning. Clearly, then, we need to have a view of text as hierarchically organized if we are to understand anaphora.

5.5 Anaphora in the environment of same-gender referents

We will see in this discussion, as in the preceding section, that simple introduction of another referent does not necessarily produce "ambiguity"; rather, it is the structural organization of the text that determines what will count as "interfering" and what not.

The pattern of anaphora for same-gender environments is close to the pattern for different-gender environments, with a few more restrictions that will be discussed in detail below:

A pronoun is used in a same-gender environment if the relevant proposition is in an active state. Otherwise, a full NP is used.

As this formulation stands, the same-gender environment seems identical to the different-gender environment; however, as will be shown below, there are a few differences.

5.5.1   Pronominalization in the active pattern

As before, included under the active pattern are basically (1) propositions whose R-structure partners are being developed, and (2) propositions that are being tied to by a return pop. I examine the first of these below.

Pronominalization is possible in an R-structure partner if two same-gender referents are mentioned in the same proposition under the following conditions:

(*a*)   if the referent mentioned in the second proposition was the grammatical subject of the first proposition (or the possessor in a nominalization); or

(*b*)   if the referent mentioned in the second proposition was not the grammatical subject of the first proposition, but *is* mentioned in the next highest nucleus.

Examples illustrating the first pattern (subject→ pronoun) are given below. (Examples are from *A House of Lions* unless otherwise indicated.)

This is not to say that Virginia's rivalry with Vanessa had diminished. *She* oscillated between abasement and respect.

Old Leslie Stephen sat now in Thoby's rooms in the Trinity Great Court. One by one the young tried to talk to *him*.

Lytton could hardly undertake the entire history of Warren Hastings. *He* would focus on

Quentin Bell has pointed to an interesting slip of the pen Virginia made in a letter to her friend Violet Dickinson. *She* begins by saying

Clive asked Lytton to join the luncheon party. *He* was a little put out to learn that Lytton had already met Desmond

While FitzGerald doesn't have a quarrel with this year's grand marshal, union leader Teddy Gleason, *he* is annoyed by the selection of IRA fugitive Michael O'Rourke as honorary grand marshal. (*People*, March 19, 1984)

Examples illustrating the second pattern follow.

Desmond once remarked that Lytton's friendships at Cambridge were more like loves. One thinks of *him* as taking possession

Desmond gave him the Oxford miniature Shakespeare and four volumes of Milton, so that *he* would carry into remote parts the immortal utterances of the English tongue.

There are also situations in which *both* same-gender referents can be referred to with pronouns.[15] This anaphoric pattern arises only when role continuity of subject is maintained; that is, the pronoun which is the subject of the clause in question must be coreferential with the subject of the clause of the R-structure partner. From a use-determines-context viewpoint, we could say that the writer signals to the reader, with the use of two pronouns, that these pronouns should be interpreted as maintaining the grammatical roles of the active proposition.

Examples of this pattern are given below.

Lytton had written an earlier essay on Hastings. *He* had seen *him* as a "superman"

In the phantasmagoria of her inner world, Virginia loved Vanessa. *She* wanted total possession of *her*.

The active pattern covers about 82 per cent of the pronouns in the environment of same-gender referents.

Another organization in which pronouns can be used in a same-gender environment is the List return pop. In this situation, two mentions of the same person, X, can be separated by references to another, same-gender, person, Y, and the second mention of person X can be done with a pronoun if and only if the second mention of X is a return pop to another member of a List structure (or a proposition containing a mention of X) and the popped-over adjunct is (*a*) also a member of the List structure and (*b*) structurally simple. Schematically, this pattern would appear thus:

Issue

X   List

X   Y   X (pronoun)

Notice that the restrictions on pronominalization in return pops are somewhat greater for same-gender environments than for different-gender environments: for the latter, pronominalization in return pops is not confined to Lists. This greater restrictedness on pronominalization seems intuitively reasonable, given the greater competition among same-gender referents for a gender-marked pronoun. This pattern covers about 12 per cent of the pronouns in the environment of same-gender referents.

Examples of the pattern of pronominalization in List return pops, with their diagrams, are given below.

(1) We see many Vanessas in the portraits that remain of her, especially those painted by Duncan Grant.

(2)   The young face was smooth, with firmly lined brows and liquid gray-green eyes.

(3)   She had sensuous lips.

(4)   She rarely used makeup.

(5)   Somewhere Virginia speaks of "her passionate mouth."

(6)   *Her* voice was beautifully modulated;

(7)   her words were carefully paced. (*A House of Lions*, p. 78)

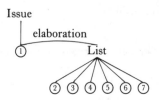

In this case the proposition containing the italicized pronoun is not an adjunct of the immediately preceding proposition (*somewhere Virginia speaks* . . .) but is another in a series of adjuncts (in a List structure) on the first line (*We see many Vanessas* . . .). The return with a pronoun is possible in spite of the presence of a same-gender referent, according to the hypothesis proposed here, because the relevant mention of Vanessa comes in a next member of a list, popping over the previous member of the list to the proposition *We see many Vanessas* . . . ; in addition the popped-over list member is structurally simple.

The next example comes from later in the same list.

(1)   We see many Vanessas in the portraits that remain of her, especially those painted by Duncan Grant.

(2)   The young face was smooth, with firmly lined brows and liquid gray-green eyes.

(3)   She had sensuous lips.

(4)   She rarely used makeup.

(5)   Somewhere Virginia speaks of "her passionate mouth."

(6)   *Her* voice was beautifully modulated;

(7)   her words were carefully paced.

(8)   Virginia, so often her historian, likens her to a bowl of golden water which brims but never overflows – or, as we have seen, to the sedate volcano.

(9)   In another image *she* has a "queer antique simplicity of surface."

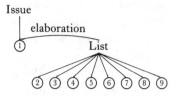

Here again we have a return in a List structure at proposition 9 done with a pronoun, in spite of an apparently "interfering" same-gender referent (which appears in proposition 8).

Another example is given below.

(1) He [i.e. Leonard] saw with child-like wonder and horror a brawling London whose violence and ginmill sordidness were visible at all times.

(2) At night he heard a woman's shrieks;

(3) or he saw a drunken, tattered man staggering about with a policeman violently hitting him;

(4) *he* also glimpsed inferno-slums filled with strange human shapes. (*A House of Lions*, p. 23)

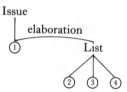

In this passage, although two other same-gender referents are mentioned in proposition 3, Leonard is pronominalized in proposition 4, and this fact correlates with the fact that proposition 4 is another member of a List structure.

It is interesting to note that, from the reader's perspective, this pattern is possible only if the reader maintains some expectation that the nucleus will soon be returned to when s/he encounters one member of the List with a same-gender referent. It is probably the case that as this List member grows in complexity, the expectation of immediate return diminishes; hence the writer risks a possible misinterpretation if a pronoun is used for a return after a structurally complex adjunct.

In this preceding section I have demonstrated that pronouns can be used even when other referents of the same gender are present if certain structural conditions hold. It is thus not the case that the simple presence of another, same-gender, referent in the neighboring clauses automatically induces the use of a full NP; rather, there is a delicate interaction between the presence of same-gender referents and the hierarchic structure of the text, and it is this interaction which determines when a pronoun can be used (and hence which determines what is to count as semantically "ambiguous"). It is critical, then, that a hierarchic approach to anaphora be adopted.

5.5.2   Full NP elsewhere

Full NPs are used whenever the circumstances described above are not met. Some of the cases in which the circumstances are not met are described below.

If two same-gender referents are mentioned in a proposition and one of them is mentioned in that proposition's R-structure partner, then a full NP will be used for the reference in the second proposition if the referent did not fill the subject role in the first proposition and was also not mentioned in the next highest nucleus. Examples illustrating this pattern appear below.

But Lytton could not control Clive's appetite for life. *Clive* was a hungry-for-experience heterosexual. (*A House of Lions*, p. 45)

It's not for nothing that Kennedy hagiographer Theodore Sorenson is a co-chairman of Hart's campaign. As *Hart*'s caravan sped onward . . . (*People*, March 26, 1984)

Keynes . . . could outplay Lytton. All *Lytton* could do was (*A House of Lions*, p. 119)

She had lied to keep shock and suffering from her [Violet]. But *Violet*, 18 years older, needed no such defence. (*A House of Lions*, p. 136)

Furthermore, if the following situation holds, in which a referent (and only that referent) is mentioned in an R-structure and then another, same-gender, referent is mentioned in the R-structure partner, then a full NP is used for the reference in the second proposition, regardless of that referent's status in higher R-structures. In this case, since the referent in the first proposition is in the active pattern, a pronoun would be heard as referring to it, rather than to the referent currently being mentioned in the second proposition (even if the latter is mentioned only two clauses back). Examples of this phenomenon follow.

Elvis had his gilded belt, Elton his spectacular spectacles and now Michael Jackson has that glittering glove. Rhinestones a-twinkling, the glove lends its wearer a magical air – as if he could pluck a rabbit from a hat with the same ridiculous ease

that he snatched an unprecedented eight Grammy awards a couple of weeks back. . . . [most of two paragraphs omitted]
Whitten says that Jackson owns six of the gloves, including two that are black and one that is red, white and blue.

Though Michael is mum about explaining why he wears the glove, other than to say it makes him feel "never offstage," *Whitten* maintains it is an integral part of the 25-year-old singer's mystique. (*People*, March 19, 1984)

In this passage, Whitten is referred to with a full NP because of the same-gender referent in the R-structure partner (*Michael*, in the pre-posed adjunct).

Another example follows.

(1) Virginia's characterizations were a matter of moods.
(2) Sometimes *Vanessa* was "marmoreally chaste" – loaded words suggesting coldness, concreteness, smoothness of surface, virginal severity.
(3) *Vanessa* has "a genius for stating unpleasant truths in her matter of fact voice." (*A House of Lions*, p. 79)

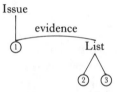

This passage is particularly interesting in that it shows what happens when two propositions (in a List structure) are adjuncts to a same-gender nucleus. In each case, Vanessa is referred to with a full NP *because* Virginia, rather than Vanessa, appears in the nucleus, and each List member in a sense cycles back to that nucleus. The proposition containing the mention of Virginia is thus active, and so is the source of referents for pronominalization. This passage is thus the exact inverse of the passage given below, in which all of the List members are done with pronouns because their referent (Vanessa) appears in the relevant nucleus (and is, therefore, in the active pattern):

(1) We see many Vanessas in the portraits that remain of her, especially those painted by Duncan Grant.
(2) The young face was smooth, with firmly lined brows and liquid gray-green eyes.
(3) She had sensuous lips.

(4)   She rarely used makeup.
(5)   Somewhere Virginia speaks of "her passionate mouth."
(6)   *Her* voice was beautifully modulated;
(7)   her words were carefully paced. (*A House of Lions*, p. 78)

It is an interesting fact about the distribution of anaphora in same-gender environments that a List return over a same-gender referent can be done with a pronoun, while a same-R-structure reference must be done with a full NP. That is, in the following structure a pronoun can be used,

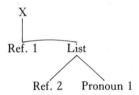

while in this structure a full NP must be used:

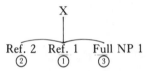

How can we account for this apparently anomalous distribution? My guess is that the List structure sets up such strong expectations that another mention of the referent is coming up that even an intervening same-gender referent does not displace the first referent from its pronominalizable position. In any other situation (at least for the type of text I examined), the expectations of a next reference are not strong enough to guarantee an accurate resolution of a pronoun, so writers avoid pronouns in such situations.

While considering the cognitive side of this difference, we should not ignore the very real – and possibly non-functionally based – influence of genre on anaphoric patterning. The observed difference between same-gender anaphora in Lists and in other structures may have more to do with the somewhat arbitrary conventions of the expository, people-oriented texts that I have used in this study than with the cognitive processes of the reader (or the writer's assumptions about those processes). As we will see in Chapter 6, the patterns of anaphora exhibited by expository texts are very much more conservative than would be indicated by cognitive processes (if the latter can be inferred from the spontaneous conversations examined in Chapter 3); the expository situation may thus have its sources in something as mundane (for linguists) as generic conventions (whose own sources are unknown).

Return pops other than in List structures provide another same-gender context in which full NPs are used. An example of this pattern is presented below.

(1) Theodore L. Hullar has been appointed executive vice chancellor at Riverside, succeeding Carlton R. Bovell.

(2) Bovell announced his resignation to return to full-time duties as a biology professor and researcher on campus.

(3) *Hullar* is director of the Agricultural Experiment Station and director for research at Cornell University. (*University Bulletin*, January 16, 1984)

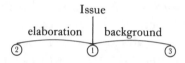

The return at proposition 3 pops over the mention of a same-gender referent in proposition 2, but proposition 3 does not pop back to an ongoing List structure; the return pop is done with a full NP.

5.5.3 Interim summary

In this section we have examined the ways in which other referents influence patterns of anaphora. The basic pattern for other-referent environments appears to be more restricted than the pattern for environments without other "interfering" referents in that only the *active* pattern seems to hold: that is, referents in propositions whose R-structure partner is being developed are available for pronominalization – any relationship more embedded than that induces the use of a full NP.

It is important to reiterate that the mere presence of another referent – whether same-gender or different-gender – is not the issue here; the crucial factors for anaphora have to do with the structural patterning of the clauses (and also in some cases the grammatical roles of the NPs in question). This critical feature of anaphora accounts for the lack of success some researchers have experienced in quantifying referent ambiguity and its effect on anaphora (see Givón 1983). Before we begin quantifying ambiguity, we need to explore qualitatively, as I have tried to do here, the structural factors that influence anaphoric patterning.

5.6   Non-structural factors

In the preceding sections I have tried to describe the patterns of anaphora in my texts that appear to have a structural basis; that is, it is the rhetorical relation of the propositions that in these instances determines what anaphoric device will be used. In this section I will present some patterns that reflect non-structural (i.e. not related to rhetorical structures) bases.

5.6.1   Further description with a full NP

As Schegloff (p. c) has pointed out, any next reference to a person is a place where further information about that person can be added. In my expository texts, this fact is often realized through the use of a full NP – complete with modifiers – in situations in which a pronoun would have been possible according to the structural patterns presented earlier. This technique is especially widely used in short articles, in which space is at a premium, and therefore any piece of information that can be packaged in a modifier or relative clause (instead of a full sentence) will appear in this "condensed" form, as part of a full NP (Dillon 1981, suggests that this strategy is used to "add more information about the thing, semicovertly, as it were" (p. 99)). Examples of this phenomenon follow.

There was one whose passion for literature was imparted to the small boy. *Mr. Floyd* made Leonard "dimly aware that lessons – things of the mind – could be exciting and even amusing." (*A House of Lions*, p. 23)

Here the full NP is used to introduce a previously unknown name for a character that was already introduced (*one*). I do not mean to claim that this is the only reason that a full NP is used here – the structural principle discussed in section 5.3 on demarcating rhetorical units may also be involved; I mean to suggest only that at least part of the motivation for using a proper noun in this passage may be what I have called the "further information" function of full NPs.

He was rescued Sunday after crawling to the top of the ravine, where he collapsed and was spotted by hikers.
    "They told me their names," he said. "I forgot them, but I'll never forget their faces."
    The lance corporal was on leave from his job as a small-arms repairman at Camp Pendleton. (*Los Angeles Times*, July 26, 1983)

Before this passage, we did not know that Bell was a lance corporal, a fact that may be significant in judging how well he performed under the stressful conditions of his accident. This information is brought in not through a complete clause, but through an anaphoric device – a full NP.

George R. Tilton, professor of geological sciences who trained as a chemist, applies chemical theories and analytical methods to geological problems. These problems concern especially the age, origin and evolution of the earth, the moon and the solar system.
   Tilton, a member of the National Academy of Sciences, is regarded as a leader in lead isotope geochemistry. (*University Bulletin*, December 1, 1980)

Bell, once a restaurant worker in his hometown of Battle Creek, Mich., said, "I thought about all the food."
   Bell, who has taken mountain survival training with the Marines, said he will continue to enjoy the woods. (*Los Angeles Times*, July 26, 1983)

In these passages again, full NPs are used in conjunction with reduced pieces of added information (non-restrictive relative clauses). The slots could have been filled with a pronoun (by the rules of return pop for the environment of no "interfering" referents) or with full NPs (by the rules of rhetorical unit demarcation); but we can say again that at least part of the reason for using a full NP in these cases is the fact that "piggyback" information is being brought in here in the form of relative clauses, and a full NP is required for the syntactic environment Referent + relative clause.

5.6.2   Classification

Another communicative situation in which a full NP can be used in the place of an expected pronoun is when the membership of the referent in a category is the facet of the referent being stressed. For example, in positions where one could have expected a pronoun, one finds *the young girl*, *the Swede*, etc. Illustrations of this pattern are given below.

Leonard Woolf sat for the scholarship examination at Trinity College – the college of Isaac Newton – in Cambridge in March 1899, when he was almost nineteen. He was adept at passing exams. In October of that year, when the century had reached an extremity of old •ge, *the right-thinking and stoical-skeptical young Jew* went up to the university. (*A House of Lions*, p. 26)

Clive goes on to tell us in this passage (which we can read only as autobiography, so closely does it fit what we know): "He had learnt to feel; and because, to feel, a man must live, it was good to be alive. I know an erudite and intelligent man, a man whose arid life had been little better than one long cold in the head, for whom the madman, Van Gogh, did nothing less." This his closest friends apparently did not grasp. *The vain little "name dropper" Clive Bell* had had a revelation. (*A House of Lions*, p. 32)

He saw with childlike wonder and horror a brawling London whose violence and ginmill sordidness were visible at all times. At night he heard a woman's shrieks; or he saw a drunken, tattered man staggering about with a policeman violently hitting him; he also glimpsed inferno-slums filled with strange human shapes. They made *the small boy* sick with terror. (*A House of Lions*, pp. 22–3)

In all of these passages, full NPs are used to categorize the referents, rather than just establish the referent's identity for the reader.

The difference between this pattern and the previous non-structural pattern lies in the newness of the information conveyed by the modification: in the first pattern ("further information"), the reader is given, in a densely packaged form, new information about the referent; in the second pattern ("classification"), already-known information is used to bring out the membership-in-a-category facet of the referent's identity. For example, we knew before reading the passages given above that Leonard was a "young Jew" and that Clive Bell tended to be thought of as a name-dropper, and that the person in London (Leonard Woolf) was a young boy.

It is a curious fact about this particular pattern of anaphora that it tends to occur mainly in literary texts (while the "further information" pattern occurs in all text-types, although concentrated in short articles). Perhaps the use of this device, since it does little in the way of hard-core information conveying, carries a flavor of flowery variation that is more typical of literary texts than, say, short articles in a university bulletin.

5.6.3   Comparison and contrast

It is very often the case that a reference will be done with a full NP if the referent is being contrasted or compared, either implicitly or explicitly, with other people. Examples from *A House of Lions* are given below.

He [Leonard] also describes how he learned to be the kind of "I" who watches himself as if he were double – "not I." This kind of self-awareness has been sketched by many others, not least Emerson and William James in their "me" and "not me." In *Leonard* it seemed as if he were both actor and observer: "I cannot avoid continually watching myself playing a part on the stage." (p. 24)

His [Clive's] laughter was an explosive spasm or guffaw, and in his youth he possessed distinct crudities that made him seem like some young rural squire out of Fielding rather than a sensitive poetry-conscious undergraduate at an ancient college. Leonard Woolf's early environment had been that of a middle-class intellectual and of a city-bred boy. *Arthur Clive Heward Bell*'s was middle-class hunting and fishing. (p. 27)

School for Lytton was erratic as well as erotic: his mother worried about his health; she was determined to ease his life. Unlike Leonard, unlike Clive, who were hearty, healthy boys, who loved games and learned their Latin and Greek well, and were heterosexuals, *Lytton* was not subjected to formal public schools. (p. 37)

At the end of his [Maynard Keynes's] time at Eton, he lived in the school as if it were his own fine country house and cooperated with his friends in running it. Unlike Leonard, Clive and Lytton, sons of suburb, countryside, metropolis, *John Maynard Keynes* was "all" Cambridge. (p. 48)

The claim being made here is that the use of the (italicized) full NP in each passage is motivated, at least in part, by the comparative or contrastive nature of its proposition. I do not mean to imply that this is the only motivation for using a full NP in all of these cases (for example, the last passage is also an illustration of "further information," since it offers the first use of the name of the person under discussion); but the comparative/contrastive aspect needs to be taken into account if we are to explain the full range of anaphoric patterning in expository texts.

In the preceding sections I have presented some types of non-structure-oriented communicative functions which seem to favor the use of full NP.[16] The underlying proposal of this presentation has been that, while hierarchic structure relations are crucial in the patterning of anaphora in written English texts, they are not responsible for every use of all the anaphoric devices that are available to us in English; some of these uses have other communicative functions as their source. These non-structural uses of various anaphoric devices have been ignored in recent discourse analysis, especially with regard to written material, so it is important that they be recognized in a full treatment of anaphora.

5.7 Summary

In this chapter I have identified and described various patterns of anaphora in written expository English. It was claimed that the most basic pattern is the *active* pattern, since it holds for different-gender and same-gender environments, as well as for environments with no "interfering" referents. The other, somewhat less common, pattern is the *controlling* pattern, and this holds only for environments with no interfering referents.

In order to understand the few instances of semi-long-distance pronominalization in the texts, I identified a structural organization called *return pop*. With a return pop the writer returns, not to the immediately preceding proposition but to another, usually superordinate, proposition. I proposed that under certain circumstances return pops can be done with pronouns; these circumstances have to do with the structure of the "popped-over" material, the content of that material, and whether there are other referents present.

It was also demonstrated that there is another set of organizing principles which can cause a full NP to be used where, according to the basic patterns of anaphora described, a pronoun would have been appropriate. These principles were shown to involve the demarcation of rhetorical units, such that a full NP is used at the beginning of a new rhetorical unit (otherwise a pronoun is used).

Finally, I tried to indicate that anaphora is not governed entirely by rhetorical organization – that there are non-structural factors which influence the choice of anaphoric device. These factors include categorization of the referent, further information about the referent, and comparison and contrast of the referent with other people.

6 *Anaphora in expository written and conversational English*

6.1 Introduction

In the preceding chapters I have explored the distribution of pronouns and full NPs in written (expository) and conversational (non-narrative) English. In this chapter I present a comparison of the anaphoric patterns found in the conversational and written texts, including same- and different-gender environments. Before beginning the presentation, however, a note about past research on the differences between spoken and written language is in order.[1]

6.2 Theories of the differences between spoken and written language

A fair amount of attention has been directed recently to the differences in syntactic structure exhibited by the two modalities (see, for example, Keenan and Bennett 1977; Ochs 1979b; Chafe 1982; Biber 1983; Akinnaso 1982; O'Donnell 1974; Tannen 1982; Rubin 1980). Claims have been made that written texts tend to be characterized by greater complexity of syntactic structure (greater use of nominalizations and complex verb structures, for example), more frequent use of subordination, and a predominance of subject–predicate structure rather than topic–comment (or reference–proposition); that is, in general there seems to be a greater degree of what Chafe (1982) calls syntactic *integration* in written texts than in spoken texts.

It should be noted at this point that the characteristics of spoken and written language that have been studied are *surface* phenomena that can be counted, and from which contrastive frequencies can be given. In this case, where absolute frequency is the distinguishing factor, the exact nature of the texts is critical: the length of the text, its level of formality, its genre, the social class of its creator, etc., can all critically influence the number of times a particular syntactic construction gets used. In the present study, on the other hand, I have examined recurrent underlying patterns of rhetorical/ interactional structure within each mode, and have isolated correlations between these recurrent structural patterns and recurrent anaphoric patterns. These structural patterns appear regardless of such factors as length of text, level of formality, or social class of author/speaker (although they may be more frequent in one particular subtype of the genre), and the correlations with linguistic coding recur. Within this paradigm, it is thus possible to make justifiable claims about the differences between certain written and certain "spoken" texts without exploring the variables mentioned above. For me, then, the method adopted in this work proves to be much more satisfactory than the surface phenomenon approach taken by previous studies.[2]

In order to draw interesting conclusions about the difference in anaphoric patterning across the modes, it is essential that the text-types chosen to represent each mode be comparable. In the recent literature on written and spoken language, various suggestions have been made for determining what constitutes comparable texts across the written–spoken division. One suggestion (see Akinnaso 1982) states that the texts must be identical in all respects except whether they are produced by the mouth or the pen; that is, to be comparable, two texts must be produced by the same person, exhibit the same degree of planning, exhibit the same degree of formality, exhibit the same degree of interactiveness (i.e., both must be monologue or both must be dialogue), and be of the same genre (story or essay, for example). This suggestion suffers from several problems: it renders naturally occurring data virtually useless, since any two such natural texts will differ on more points than the instrument with which they were produced; it sees texts as reducible to a set of controllable variables, and hence oversimplifies the extremely complex nature of text production and comprehension; and it presupposes that we want to explain the differences between written and oral texts using the controllable variables established, and not that we might first be interested in simply describing the differences.

Another suggestion, which I find more appealing, states that there are marked and unmarked types of text for each modality, and that we should compare texts of the same markedness (see Biber 1983). For example, multi-party spontaneous conversation is the unmarked text-type for oral production, and expository prose is one of the unmarked text-types for written (what Biber calls 'literate') production. This way of looking at genre and modality seems to me to be highly appropriate, since it allows us to compare what one typically does when writing with what one typically does when speaking:

. . . There is no a priori reason why "functionally equivalent" tasks are in fact "comparable" across the two modes. In a comparison of academic expository prose and academic lectures, for example, we might find few linguistic differences, and be tempted to conclude that speech utilizes "literate strategies" and thereby confirm the view that there are not major differences between speech and writing. But this conclusion would ignore the fact that lectures, although spoken, are not typical of the spoken mode. . . . Thus, even though a study of this type would control for communicative factors, from one perspective it would not be based on comparable tasks. Rather, it would contrast a typical written task with a highly untypical spoken task. (Biber 1983: 9)

In light of this discussion, I have chosen to use Biber's notion of comparability as a basis for choosing "comparable" texts. For the present study I have selected a large group of expository monologic written texts from a range of sources which are compared, with respect to anaphora, with naturally occurring conversations among friends and/or relatives.

We can now turn to a comparison of the anaphoric patterns in the written and conversational texts.

6.3 The basic patterns

The basic patterns of each mode were described as follows:

For non-story conversation:

The first mention of a referent in a sequence is done with a full NP. After that, by using a pronoun the speaker displays an understanding that the sequence has not been closed down.

For expository writing:

A pronoun can be used to refer to a person if there is a previous mention of that person in a proposition that is active or controlling; otherwise a full NP is used.

We could say for both of these discourse-types that a mention can be done with a pronoun if the referent is in focus (Grosz 1977), in consciousness (Chafe 1976; Dillon 1981; Reichman 1981), textually evoked (Prince 1981) or high in topicality (Givón 1983), where these terms can be operationally defined in terms of the discourse structure. That is, we could say that a referent is a topic, or in focus, or in consciousness if it has been mentioned in a sequence which is open or active or controlling (this is, in essence, how

Grosz and Reichman use the terms they have chosen). This would provide a clear definition for terms, especially topic and focus, that have otherwise been tossed about in rather loose ways (see Gundel 1974 for a history of the term *topic*, and Prince 1981 for a discussion of the notion of givenness).[3] It should be noted, however, that if these concepts are to be defined according to discourse structure (as indeed they must be), then we must be aware that they will mean something different for each discourse-type, since by convention each discourse-type has "chosen" a different unit within which these concepts are situated.

The main difference between the patterns for conversation and expository prose lies in the distinction between the notions *closed*, on the one hand, and *active* or *controlling*, on the other. In particular, we saw that there were instances of extremely long-distance pronominalization in the conversational material because the level of embedding and the nature of the embedding seemed to have little influence on anaphora; in the expository material, on the other hand, there were no clear patterns of extremely long-distance pronominalization, and the level of embedding turned out to be crucial for anaphora. Basically, after one level of embedding, the written material required that a full NP be used.

The long-distance aspect of the anaphora patterns in these two groups of texts is particularly interesting, since both types allow return pops (a large source of the long-distance pronominalization in the conversational material), but they have substantially different constraints on the association of return pops with pronouns: for the conversational data (same-gender environments aside), pronominalization with a return pop is essentially unconstrained – that is, it can apply in any structural context – while for the written data, pronominalization with a return pop was governed by the following restrictions:

1   The popped-over material contains mention of the relevant referent; or
2   the popped-over material must be structurally non-complex.

The constraints on embedding and pronominalization are equally disparate. In the conversational material, long-distance pronominalization is possible even in deeply embedded utterances; in the written material, however, pronominalization requires that at most one level of embedding be present, regardless of the nature of the surrounding text.

Quantitative data supporting these differences are presented in Tables 6.1 and 6.2 below. The figures indicate the average distance to the most recent mention of a given referent for the anaphoric device in question,[4] and

Table 6.1 *Referential distance in conversational and written texts (for pronouns only)*

	Referential distance (in clauses)
Conversational	2.52
Written	1.21

Table 6.2 *Proportion of each anaphoric device*

	Full NP		Pronoun		Total
Conversational	87	(22%)	306	(78%)	393
Written	548	(47%)	608	(53%)	1,156

the proportion of each anaphoric device in the two text types. Although, as we saw in Chapters 3 and 5, the most recent mention of a referent is not always the relevant antecedent mention, for conformity with the counting procedures developed in Givón 1983 I have adopted the most recent mention as the critical reference. The results suggest that (*a*) full NPs are much more prevalent in expository written texts than they are in conversational texts, and (*b*) the referential distance for pronouns is much greater in the conversational texts than it is in the written texts. Long-distance pronominalization – either of the embedding type or of the return pop type – is thus basically non-existent in the written texts. There is thus no single abstract pattern with which we could associate terms like topic, focus, or consciousness (see Fox, forthcoming, b, for a fuller discussion of this point). Even for the basic pattern there are too many differences, brought about by convention and channel limitations (Dillon 1981), to allow us to formulate a unifying strategy of anaphora.[5]

6.3.1 Continuity and anaphora in written and conversational texts

In the discussions of data in Chapters 3 and 5, I tried to indicate points at which the traditional theory of anaphora (represented by Givón 1983) falls short of accounting for the patterns of anaphora exhibited by the texts chosen. The criticisms leveled against the traditional theory are extremely strong in the case of the conversational data: long-distance pronominalization is common (some researchers have recorded gaps of up to 30 minutes), and full NPs can be used in situations where distance would have predicted a pronoun. In this case, it is entirely clear that a structural approach to texts is critical for our understanding of anaphora.

The criticisms brought against the traditional theory in the case of the written data are not so strong, however: we saw that real long-distance pronominalization probably does not occur (the longest gap in my data being five clauses), and in a few instances the conditions on pronominalization require circumstances that imply a more string-oriented view of texts than I am advocating. For example, pronominal return pops exhibit limitations on complexity of the material popped over (which can be read as a limitation on distance), but this limitation on complexity can be overcome if there are mentions of the relevant referent in the popped-over material (which can also be read as a function of distance). Should we then abandon the structural approach for the written texts and accept the traditional theory? If not, what should we say about anaphora in written texts to account for its apparently more linear nature?[6]

I firmly believe that the answer to the first question is negative: we did see that full NPs occur where distance would have predicted pronouns, and the gaps that do occur fall into structural patterns which can be described using rhetorical structure analysis; furthermore, the notion of "interfering" referent can only be accurately described in terms of structure. So we can be sure that a structural approach illuminates some large portion of the data that would otherwise remain opaque. We are thus left with the question of the somewhat more linear nature of anaphora in written texts: how are we to account for the fact that distance (or something like it) does seem to play a role in the written texts, while it is minimally important in conversational texts?

I currently have no definite answer to this question. Since the modes differ in respect of more than one feature (having different values at least for formality, plannedness, modality, genre, and number of contributing participants), it is impossible to say exactly which feature, or which function, contributes most to the greater dominance of something like distance in the written texts. As an initial guess, however, I would like to suggest that the stability of a written text over the period of reading might make a significant difference in the treatment of anaphora. If we compare return pops across the modes, the difference will be clear. In conversation, we saw that a return pop "closes off" the popped-over material, and since there is no remaining physical trace of that now-closed material, the interlocutors are free to forget its content.[7] In written texts, on the other hand, there is a very obvious set of physical traces remaining of the closed-off material, traces which the reader's eye may return to; hence the reader is less likely to forget the material. Perhaps because of the traces, then, the intervening material assumes a greater importance in the attention of the reader than it does when there are no physical traces, and as a result what appears to be distance assumes a correspondingly greater importance for anaphora (Dillon 1981; Rubin 1980).

A note of caution regarding such explanations is in order, however. As I have shown elsewhere (Fox, forthcoming, a), not all genres of written text show such conservative (and possibly distance-influenced) patterns of anaphora; the patterns exhibited by written narratives, for example, more closely resemble the patterns of the conversational texts than those of the expository texts. It must thus be conceded that it is not just the physical facts of writing that influence anaphora; the conventions established for each written genre are also critical in the process.[8]

6.4   Demarcating structural units

In Chapter 5, we saw that full NPs in expository written texts are often used at the beginning of rhetorical units where pronouns could have been appropriate. Such a claim was also made for the conversational material, but there the pattern was shown to be relatively minor. In Table 6.3, I have presented indirect evidence that this pattern is extremely widespread in

Table 6.3 *Full NP and non-anaphoric functions*

	Referent in preceding clause		Referent not in preceding clause		Total
Written					
Full NP	207	(38%) (29%)	341	(62%) (78%)	548
Pronoun	513	(84%) (71%)	95	(16%) (22%)	608
Total	720		436		1,156
Conversational					
Full NP	10	(11%) (6%)	77	(89%) (33%)	87
Pronoun	151	(49%) (94%)	155	(51%) (67%)	306
Total	161		232		393

Note: The first percentage figure in each pair reads across (e.g. 207 is 38% of 548), the second reads down (e.g. 207 is 29% of 720).

expository written texts and not at all common in the conversational texts. The results show clearly the differences between the two types. Even when the referent is mentioned in the immediately preceding clause, 29 per cent of the time (207/720) a full NP is used in the written material, whereas in the same situation in the conversational texts full NPs are used only 6 per cent of the time (10/161). These findings indicate that full NPs in the written texts are doing much more than just the standard referent-tracking work attributed to them: that is, if they occur even when their antecedent is plainly retrievable from the preceding clause, then they are not simply performing an anaphoric duty. Rather, they are helping to block the text into its structural units.[9] This function could not be as common in the conversational texts as in the written, given the low percentage of references in this situation done with full NPs.

Furthermore, Table 6.3 suggests that a larger percentage of the full NPs in the written texts occur under these conditions – i.e., referent mentioned in preceding clause – than in the conversational texts: 38 per cent (207/548) of all the full NPs in the written texts occurred under these conditions, compared to 11 per cent (10/87) for the conversational material. Here again we see that, while the structuring function of full NPs is prevalent in the written texts, it is much less so in the conversational texts.

It is interesting that written texts seem, on the one hand, to be more sensitive than conversational texts to some type of linear distance and, on the other hand, also to be more sensitive to hierarchic units. These sensitivities do not contradict one another; rather, they both indicate an awareness of the extremely important role of the writer's explicitness in guiding the reader to the intended interpretation of the text (since the reader can never ask for clarification, and cannot use prosodic information as a clue): the first sensitivity guides the reader to an interpretation of an anaphor that s/he might not have been able to make because of interfering physical "traces"; the second sensitivity guides the reader to an interpretation of the structure of the text that s/he might not otherwise have been able to make owing to lack of structural "signposts" from the writer.

6.5   Different-gender referents and anaphora

In Chapter 3, I proposed that pronominalization in the environment of a different-gender referent in the conversational data is quite free. That is, a return pop over material containing mentions of a different-gender referent was seen to be done with a pronoun; and if two referents of different genders appeared in the same adjacency pair, then a mention of either one of them in a "tying" pair could be done with a pronoun. Furthermore, a pronoun could be used to refer to a person in a second-pair part even if that person was not mentioned in the first-pair part of the pair but was mentioned in the tied-to pair:

H. So: en she already wrote him about me en everyth//ing
    en she'd li:ke=
N. Awr::ight.
H. =(t') fix us u:p.
    ·
    ·
    ·
N. Well wt's ( ) he li://ke.
H. ·hhhhhhhh a-ah: she says ( ) he y'know
    th'las'time she saw him

In this passage we get a female-gender pronoun in the second-pair part even though its referent does not appear in the first-pair part of the sequence. The proposed reason for this distribution is the fact that the relevant referent appeared in the tied-to pair.

In Chapter 5, on the other hand, I suggested that pronominalization in the written material in the environment of different-gender referents was fairly restricted, being limited to the following conditions:

1 If both referents are mentioned in the same proposition, then either one of them can be pronominalized in the R-structure partner.
2 In a return pop situation, if the popped-over material is structurally non-complex, then the returned-to referent can be pronominalized.

The differences in distribution are discussed below.

In written expository English texts, then, we do not find a pronoun used to refer to a person in the adjunct of a structure if there is a reference to a different-gender person in the nucleus of that R-structure. This pattern differs from the situation in the conversational material in the following sense. Let me suggest that an adjacency pair and a tying pair can be seen as roughly equivalent to the nucleus of an R-structure and an embedded R-structure realization of its adjunct. That is, the following structures can be seen to be basically equivalent:

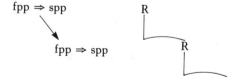

The equivalence of these structures arises from the equation of tied-to pair with nucleus and tying pair with adjunct, and the equation of an adjacency pair with an R-structure (because each is the basic unit of structure in its mode). Hence the tying adjacency pair is roughly equatable with an embedded R-structure, and the first-pair part of the adjacency pair is parallel to the nucleus of the embedded R-structure.[10]

Given this comparison, we can see that the conversational material displays a pattern of pronominalization not seen in the written material. That is, the conversational material allows a pronoun in the second-pair part of the tying pair (in the structure shown above), while the written material appears to require a full NP in the structurally equivalent adjunct of the embedded R-structure.

Return pops done with pronouns are possible in both the written and the conversational texts. The constraints on returns in the written texts are much greater, however, than they are in the conversational data. Basically, in the conversational texts I could find no constraints on return pops in the environment of different-gender referents, while in the written texts the constraints were quite strong:

A return pop can be done with a pronoun even if the popped-over adjunct mentions a different-gender referent if and only if that adjunct is structurally simple.

Here again we see that the written material exhibits a much more conservative pattern of anaphora than does the conversational data.

In Table 6.4 I present the results of some text-counts which support the structural analyses given above. It shows that in a different-gender environment the modes are skewed in exactly opposite directions with regard to anaphora: full NP is used 61 per cent (51/83) of the time in the written material, while pronoun is used 72 per cent (18/25) of the time in the conversational texts. These figures thus indirectly support the claim that the constraints on pronominalization are greater in the written texts than in the conversational texts.[11]

Table 6.4 *Anaphora in the environment of different-gender referents*

	Written		Conversational	
Full NP	51	(61%)	7	(28%)
Pronoun	32	(39%)	18	(72%)
Total	83		25	

In almost every situation, then, the written texts exhibit a more conservative pattern of anaphora in the environment of different-gender referents than do the conversational texts.

6.6 Same-gender referents and anaphora

The conservatism of the written material (with regard to anaphora) is especially apparent in the environment of same-gender referents. Here, the only situation in which pronominalization is tolerated in the written texts is if the two referents are in the same proposition; in the R-structure partner, the referent that had been in subject role in the first proposition can be pronominalized. (There are two other minor conditions in which a non-subject can be pronominalized: see section 5.5.1). Return pops with pronouns are also allowed in this environment, but only under extremely restricted conditions.

While same-gender environment is the most restricted environment for the conversational texts, it is not as constrained as the same environment in the written texts. Return pops can be done with pronouns in same-gender environment (assuming there are other linguistic devices used to guide the reader to the appropriate level of structure), and there appears to be no singling out of subject NPs for special pronominalization status.

Quantitative evidence which supports the more widespread use of full NP in the same-gender environment for the written material is given in Table 6.5. Here again we see that full NPs are much more commonly resorted to in this environment within the written texts than is the case in the conversational texts.[12]

Table 6.5 *Anaphora in the environment of same-gender referents*

	Written	Conversational
Full NP	142 (87%)	9 (43%)
Pronoun	21 (13%)	12 (57%)
Total	163	21

A full comparison of the environments of (*a*) no interfering referents, (*b*) different-gender referents, and (*c*) same-gender referents in the written and conversational texts is given in Table 6.6. Notice that, while the

Table 6.6 *Anaphora in three environments*

	No interfering referents		Different-gender		Same-gender	
Written:						
Full NP	312	(36%)	51	(61%)	142	(87%)
Pronoun	553	(64%)	32	(39%)	21	(13%)
Total	865		83		163	
Conversational:						
Full NP	16	(6%)	7	(28%)	9	(43%)
Pronoun	272	(94%)	18	(72%)	12	(57%)
Total	288		25		21	

conversational texts are obviously sensitive to these environments (reaching a level of 43 per cent use of full NP), the written texts are clearly more extreme in their response (reaching a level of 87 per cent use of full NP). It should also be noted that the percentage of full NPs used increases in a direction consonant with the structural patterns described in Chapters 3 and 5. That is, we saw that the environment of no interfering referents – where "interfering" was determined structurally – allowed the most freedom of pronominalization, the environment of different-gender referents showed a slightly more restricted distribution of pronouns, and the environment of same-gender referents showed a fairly high degree of restriction on pronominalization; in fact, the figures in Table 6.6 indicate that the percentage of full NPs increases in just this direction, as one would have expected intuitively.

6.7   Non-structural factors in anaphora

In Chapters 3 and 5, I proposed that there are factors other than structural ones that affect the anaphoric patterning in texts. That is, I was suggesting that it is not just the hierarchic organization of clauses and propositions that determines which anaphoric device will be used at any given point; rather, there are non-structural factors which also, in perhaps a secondary way, influence anaphoric choices. The non-structural factors which were claimed to be relevant for the anaphoric distribution in each of the modes are listed in Table 6.7. The factors which involve multi-party interaction are obviously excluded from the written material (this includes disagreements and replacements of utterances). The others are discussed below.

Table 6.7 *Non-structural factors in conversation and writing*

Conversational	Written
Replacement of an utterance	Further description
Disagreeing	Classification
	Comparison and contrast
Overt recognitionals	
Assessments	
Category membership	

Two of the factors which were claimed to be important in the conversational texts may also play some role in the written material, although they were not mentioned with regard to the latter. These are overt recognitionals and assessments.

We may recall that overt recognitionals are phrases which, instead of presupposing the recognition of a participant, explicitly claim that recognition as their function. Such phrases as *know X, remember X* were said to be overt recognitionals. I proposed in Chapter 3 that overt recognitionals provided an environment in which full NPs could be used when pronouns would have been predicted from the hierarchic structure.

By excluding this category of non-structural factors from the discussion on anaphora in the written texts, I did not mean to imply that such factors had no possible place in determining anaphora; on the contrary, it seems quite probable that if I could find instances of overt recognitionals, they would be seen to behave in very much the same way in the written texts as they do in the conversational texts. Unfortunately, I was unable to find examples of this type of non-structural influence in my texts.

Essentially the same situation holds for assessments. While I do not doubt that assessments in written texts can be done with full NPs, I found only one instance in all the texts that appeared to provide some empirical support for this intuition:

His greatest satisfaction . . . was his use of his power, when he became a senior boy, to put an end to offensive sexual practices in the school. "When I left for St. Paul's in 1894," he wrote with a note of distinct pride years later, "the atmosphere had changed from that of a sordid brothel to that more appropriate to fifty fairly happy small boys under the age of fourteen." *Leonard was a reformer from the first.* (*A House of Lions*, p. 23)

In this passage it seems clear that an assessment is being done with a full NP. The pattern is not widely enough documented to treat it as an established phenomenon, however, so I have not included it in the discussion of anaphora in written texts. Nonetheless, with a broader and larger database it is likely that assessment will be a strong category under non-structural factors.

One non-structural factor in the conversational data which appears to have no place in the written texts is category membership. In this case, a first mention of a referent is done with a pronoun rather than a full NP, and no fuller specification of the person's identity is necessarily forthcoming (because the exact identity is irrelevant to the interaction). I found no instances of this pattern in the written material, and I expect that there are no instances to be found. This belief is based on several different types of reasoning: first, writers and readers do not initially have enough shared knowledge to allow any given participant's identity to be thoroughly known to both parties (except, perhaps, in the case of *He* to mean God); second, in all my experience with expository prose I have no recollection of initial pronominal use which is not followed by a fuller explication of the participant's identity (suspenseful uses of initial pronouns do not count here, since the identity is eventually disclosed; here suspense, and precisely *not* anaphoric resolution, is the author's goal). We have here, then, a fairly substantive discrepancy in the use of pronouns in conversational and written texts.

The first factor which is apparent in written texts but not in my conversational texts is comparison and contrast. In the written material, I found that if two (or more) people are compared or contrasted with regard to some characteristic or feature, then both will be realized with full NPs. Although I have no examples of this factor in the conversational texts I examined, there is some reason to suspect that in fact it does operate in conversation as it does in writing: in her study of the use of *it* and *that* in spoken apartment layout narratives, Linde (1979) found that when speakers described the physical layout of their apartments, *that* was used when the speaker wished to contrast one room (or apartment) with another, even if *it* would have been expected for structural reasons. We thus have, in spoken texts, something in the direction of a full NP used in a situation of contrast. Since the modes thus probably do not differ in this respect, I will not offer any further discussion of this particular factor.

There are two additional factors which are characteristic of the written texts but do not seem to be relevant to the conversational material: Further Description and Classification.[13] These factors are not excluded absolutely from conversational interaction: but since the functions in written texts which work together to produce them are not common in conversational texts, they are not often observable. The functions which are involved in Further Description appear to be a combination of lack of space and a fair amount of information to be presented in that space. A full NP in the Further Description environment allows both of these conflicting constraints to be accommodated, since a small amount of space is used to convey a maximum load of information. Since in natural, spontaneous conversation there is only in rare instances a shortage of "space" (time) *and* a need to convey a heavy dose of information, the efficient use of a full NP in the further description mode is almost never made (I found no instances of it in my data). Furthermore, it is almost certainly the case that such use of a full NP is felt to be associated with generic conventions of particular text-types, and hence might be generically (i.e. having to do with genre) inappropriate in the context of natural conversation.

The needs filled by the full NP in the Classification environment are not clear to me: but, as I suggested in Chapter 5, they probably have something to do with stylistic variety and colorfulness of phrasing (hence this environment was found much more frequently in longer, more literary texts than in short, to-the-point texts). Although conversationalists are sensitive to variation and poetic phrasing (see Tannen 1984), they appear not to engage in selecting colorful full NPs to describe persons whose identities have already been established.[14]

We can see from this brief discussion of the differences in non-structural factors in written and conversational texts that it is the discrepancy in circumstances and communicative needs, as well as generic conventions, that determines which factors will arise in one mode and not in another. Conversation, of course, leans towards factors which involve the overt interaction of two or more interlocutors and an overt consolidation of their mutual knowledge and affect, while expository writing leans towards factors which involve the restrictions imposed on writing by lack of space and lack of mutual knowledge between the relevant parties, as well as by conventions of the mode. The differences in anaphoric patterning are thus somewhat predictable from the differences in communicative needs. Generic conventions cannot, however, be dismissed as a source of difference.

7 Conclusions

The actual reality of language-speech is not the abstract system of linguistic forms, not the isolated monologic utterance, and not the psychophysiological act of its implementation, but the social event of verbal interaction implemented in an utterance or utterances.

(Voloshinov 1973: 94)

In addition to the issues mentioned explicitly in Chapter 1, the previous chapters have raised several larger theoretical issues which I have not yet addressed. I would like to touch on two of these fundamental issues here, if only superficially, to open these concerns up for discussion. The two issues I would like to address explicitly here are the localness of linguistic patterning and the nature of discourse structure.

7.1 Localness

In Chapter 6, I raised the issue of genre-specific conventions of anaphoric patterning. As we have seen, there is no single rule for anaphora that can be specified for all of English (even the limited subset of third-person singular human examined here); instead, we have a variety of specific patterns which obviously share a number of general characteristics, but which nevertheless differ enough to require separate formulation (Fox, forthcoming, b). This is one level at which patterns are local (specific to a particular genre) rather than global (specifiable for all of English). There are other levels at which the idea of localness seems fruitful; it is to these levels that I would like to turn now.[1]

In his paper "Meaning and memory," Bolinger (1976) presents a model of language in which a single language is viewed as a "gerry-rigged" system with no overarching structure; instead, there is tight structure at a lower, local level, and only loose connections between these tightly organized local segments (this corresponds in some ways with Wittgenstein's metaphor of language as a European city). Forms are related by analogy in a pattern of family resemblance. This portrait of grammar obviously contrasts with the more traditional one offered by structuralists and formal grammarians, in which language is seen as a tightly knit set of interrelated forms.

Another view of localness appears in Sacks *et al.* 1974, in their treatment of the turn-taking system for English conversation (see Chapter 2 for details). In this piece, Sacks *et al.* postulate a set of fairly abstract rules which are said to govern turn-taking behavior in natural conversation. In spite of the abstractness of the rules, however, they suggest that turn-taking is in fact locally managed – that is, worked out each time anew in the particular situation at hand:

We have reasons to take seriously the possibility that a characterization of turn-taking organization for conversation could be developed which would have the important twin features of being context-free and capable of extraordinary context-sensitivity. . . .

One reason for expecting the existence of some such type of organization is as follows. Conversation can accommodate a wide range of situations, interactions in which persons in varieties . . . of identities are operating; it can be sensitive to the various combinations; and it can be capable of dealing with a change of situation within a situation. (Sacks *et al.* 1974: 699)

In this case, then, we have an abstract system which is actually instantiated in a highly local, context-sensitive manner.

Both of these notions of localness – locally structured and locally managed – support, and receive support from, the analyses offered here. The analyses of anaphoric patterning described in Chapters 3 and 5 support the notion of local structure by the fact that even within a single discourse-type, even for this limited domain within anaphora, it was necessary to identify as many as thirteen subpatterns – hardly a good case for an overarching principle of anaphora in English.

The analyses also support the notion of local management, in that they offer a loosely structured system of fairly abstract patterns (although not really "context-free" in the sense defined by Sacks *et al.*) which are also highly situated in their relation to real-time use. In other words, by themselves these patterns cannot predict which device will be chosen for a certain situation, because the outcome of any given anaphoric choice will be exactly fitted to the particulars of the situation, rather than to some abstract pattern. The patterns described are thus both abstract and situationally defined.

Given the importance of this interplay between local and abstract, then, we can say, following Rumelhart *et al.* 1986, that local organization is more basic in understanding language than has been assumed previously (see also Bates and MacWhinney, forthcoming; Brooks 1978; Serwatka 1986; Hopper 1986; and others working in the Connectionist paradigm: Hinton and Anderson 1981; McClelland and Rumelhart 1985); it is from this local organization that more general rules and abstractions emerge:

Schemata are not "things." There is no representational object which is a schema. Rather, schemata emerge at the moment they are needed from the interaction of large numbers of much simpler elements all working in concert with one another. Schemata are not explicit entities, but rather are implicit in our knowledge and are created by the very environment that they are trying to interpret – as it is interpreting them. (Rumelhart *et al.* 1986: 18)

This view of patterns as emergent from smaller structures represents a clear break from the philosophies of language behavior now widely accepted in linguistics and cognitive science. As such, it is a critical step forward in our understanding of linguistic behavior.

7.2   Discourse structure

It is a natural outcome of this emphasis on localness that we re-examine our notion of discourse structure. If, for example, schemata are not "things" but are emergent out of smaller units, then presumably the structure one finds in a finished text or conversation is a by-product in some way of the many smaller, locally situated units produced in real-time (see Ladefoged 1980, for a related point). This is perhaps somewhat less true of planned expository prose than of conversation, since in the former the writer has the opportunity to create something which is tightly organized; but it is still certainly true of on-line reading. It should be clear, then, that an approach which describes the structure of completed texts, and then relates that structure to the uses of anaphora, falls prey to the misrepresentations common to any approach which ignores the localness of linguistic phenomena.

The analyses of conversation presented in this study follow closely the notion of structure as emergent from the local management of small units. I have heeded Schegloff (1981: 89) in treating the orderliness of anaphora as locally managed, and achieved:

If certain stable forms appear to emerge or recur in talk, they should be understood as an orderliness wrested by the participants from interactional contingency, rather than as automatic products of standardized plans. Form, one might say, is also the distillate of action and/or interaction, not only its blueprint. If that is so, then the description of forms of behavior, forms of discourse (such as stories) included, has to include interaction among their constitutive domains.

The analyses given in Chapter 3 stress the contingency of conversational action, the interactive nature of conversational structure, and the mutual creation of discourse and grammar. In these analyses, then, the fine interplay between abstract pattern and situatedness is handled in a way consonant with the paradigm suggested by Rumelhart *et al.* and Sacks *et al.*

The analyses of expository prose presented do not quite so obviously follow this model of emergent structure. This is a result of the fact that the interplay between abstract structure and local situatedness is more complex for written texts than for conversation. In the case of written texts, there is a finished product which has been designed to be seen as an integrated whole; and yet clearly the reading process, which the writer must anticipate with the use of things like anaphoric devices, is locally situated (van Dijk and Kintsch 1983; Iser 1975) and very much a process rather than a product (Dillon 1981). In dealing with the structure of written texts, then, we must acknowledge these two aspects: text as a finished static product, and text as an emergent constructing process.[2]

The analyses I have offered for the expository data try to straddle these two aspects of written texts, on the one hand by focusing on the real-time interpretation of propositions in a text, how they are fit into small units, and how this real-time process relates to anaphora, and on the other hand by recognizing the structure of a passage as a whole, as it might have been conceived by the author. Thus the rather greater emphasis in Chapter 5 on static structural factors is not a mistake: written texts do have this product side to them that conversations do not share.[3] But the product aspect is counterbalanced by a consistent view to the reading process.

7.3   Conclusion

This model of language, which sees patterning as emergent from smaller, specific instances, and structure as emerging from the interaction of many smaller units, comes at a time when new ways of looking at language behavior, especially discourse behavior, are critical if we are to extend our understanding of the relationships between language, cognition, and society. The patterns of anaphora described in this study, in all their variety, are offered in the spirit of this new tradition of locally emergent structure, in celebration of the apparent paradox of the local yet abstract nature of linguistic behavior.

Notes

1 Introduction

1 See Partee 1984 for a somewhat different perspective on discourse anaphora.
2 For example, it turns out not to be the case that simply having another referent in the vicinity (even one of the same gender) counts as problematic for the hearer/reader.

2 Conversational analysis

1 Reichman (1981) develops a relevant method of analyzing conversation which she calls "context space theory." It is not complete enough to use for the data I examine here – it does not, for example, cover interactional units like invitations, announcements, and their various responses – but her style of analysis has been critical for some of the notions developed in Chapters 3 and 5, so it is worth giving a brief overview of her method here.

In this work, Reichman distinguishes twelve relations: support, restatement of point being supported, interruption, return after interruption, indirect challenge, direct challenge, concede subargument, prior logical abstraction, contrastive respecification, analogy, further development.

In addition, each context space – similar to Grosz's focus space – is assigned a status that reflects its current prominence in the conversation. Some of the statuses, with their definitions, are given below (Reichman 1981: 86). Reichman uses these statuses in analyzing the anaphora in her data.

Active   The context space in which the utterances currently being stated are placed. There can only be one active context space at a given point in the conversation.
Controlling The context space in direct relation to which an active context space is being developed. There can only be one controlling context space at a given point in the conversation.
Open   A previously active context space that was interrupted before completion of its corresponding communicative goal.
Closed   A context space discussion of which is believed completed for the present time.

2 For a discussion of notation as theory, see Ochs 1979a.

3 Anaphora in conversational English

1 The transcripts used here were graciously made available to me by Manny Schegloff.

2 Although this study focuses on the *distribution* of anaphoric devices, rather than on their production or resolution, the findings are very much in keeping with the conclusions on anaphoric processing offered by Tyler and Marslen-Wilson (1982: 281). Tyler and Marslen-Wilson suggest that resolution is not an all-or-none search process according to the lexical properties of the relevant pronoun; rather, it involves "multiple activation of potential antecedents":

> According to this view, the constraints on anaphor resolution that derive from the *lexical* properties of a pronoun are a relatively subsidiary aspect of the resolution process. The more dominant factor is what we have been calling pragmatic inference – those processes that assess the interpretative plausibility of potential antecedents. . . . They should not necessarily be restricted to just a single antecedent selected on the basis of other criteria, but rather should be able to operate on the wider set of potential antecedents offered by the discourse at that particular moment.

The distributions described by the present study can be seen as delimiting what the discourse offers in the way of potential antecedents. This kind of work, then, although not directly involved with resolution, furthers our understanding of what referents the hearer/reader has available for achieving resolution of a given anaphor. See also Clark and Haviland 1977 and Sanford and Garrod 1981 for a psychological perspective on resolution of discourse anaphors.

3 I have characterized the status of the sequence as "not closed," rather than "continuing," because I mean for the pattern to characterize what the sequence has come to by the time the speaker produces the anaphor in question (e.g. closed or not closed) rather than what the speaker is going to do with the sequence (e.g. continue it or start something else). This formulation is meant in part to capture the fact that speakers use full NPs to continue an already fully closed sequence. Just continuing is thus not sufficient grounds for pronominalization.

4 The fairly lengthy silences before the turn expansions in each of the following examples can be thought of as the "noise" of the turn-taking system going through its ordered rules – perhaps through more than one cycle – (until rule 1(c) is reached).

5 Throughout this discussion I will use the term *tying* to refer to the subsequent pair, and the term *tied-to* to refer to the preceding pair.

6 The observation that members of a series are at the same level of structure – rather than one being subordinate to another – is reflected in the annotations of the examples by keeping the structure-level character the same, e.g. (fpp (1,a)) and (fpp (2,a)).

7 It is also possible that S's last line is a second-pair part to H's announcement; in this case, the pronoun occurs *within* the adjacency pair. Either of these analyses is consistent with the basic pattern proposed above.

8 This fact probably does not have a significant structural basis but is rather a coincidental aspect of the data examined.

9 The term *pop* comes from the Augmented Transition Network grammar metaphor: see Reichman 1981 for a detailed discussion.

10 The pronoun in line 32 contrasts with a full NP of the form *that guy* – C could have said *What's that guy's name?*

11 I give a full explication of how this structure is achieved below.

12 B does not indicate that she has heard A's utterance as a joke. This could be a result of any of a number of factors, including the possibility that B does not want to give A the satisfaction of having made a successful "funny." In spite of B's lack of response, however, we can hear A's utterance as a joke, based on a willful misinterpretation of B's *So I'm sure they're happy about that.*

13 I am using "native intuition" here in finding the referent of *that* in B's line 18.

14 In practice, of course, this adjacency pair "chaining" is limited.

15 It is probably the case that the sort of move C makes at line 20 has a limited range of distribution; that is, it probably could not have been done successfully if G's line 12 had engendered a lengthy discussion about Sundusky track. For such a move to come off, it is almost certainly necessary for the party attempting it to nip the "interrupting" material in the bud, as it were.

16 Reichman (1981) notes that if a claim is made, after which some evidence is given to support the claim, a return to the claim will close the evidence off. Returns after interruptions are also said to close off the interrupting material.

17 Admittedly, this last mention of Little might well have been done with a full NP even if a return pop had not intervened because of the adjacency-pair "chain" that occurs between the two relevant mentions. This other possibility does not, however, negate the possibility that the return pop closes off for pronominalization the Marlon Little sequence of lines 11–21.

18 I say "presumably" because I have no evidence from my data to support, or not support, this pattern. I would expect, however, on the basis of the rest of the findings, that anaphora in different-gender environments is similar in this respect to the environment of no "interfering" referents.

19 Schegloff (1979) has noted a similar phenomenon at the beginning of new topics.

20 It is probably the case that the "Sam" mentioned at line 17 is Tucker; it cannot be conclusively shown, however, that Sam and Tucker are not two different people.

21 It is also possible that M hears that the sequence containing mention of Hawkins has been closed down by the lengthy lapse at line 41 and the talk at lines 42–8 about the weather. In this case, the full NP would reflect M's understanding that the sequence has been closed, rather than having anything to do with competing referents. In fact, both of these factors may in some sense operate at once.

22 This reference will be discussed later.

23 Reichman 1981 and Grosz 1977 are examples of analyses which do not deal with cases where pronouns would have been interpretable, but where full NPs are nonetheless used.

24 This example contains not just a simple *know*+full NP but rather full NP+*know*+pro – something like a left-dislocation (e.g. *Mary, I like her*). The

point here is that, in the context of overtly determining the recognitionality of a referent, a full NP is likely to appear.

25 The reason for starting a new unit with the marked member of an opposition (in this case, full NP) is unclear; nonetheless, it is a documentable phenomenon across languages (see Fox, forthcoming (c)).

26 Arguably one main clause and one subordinate clause.

4 Rhetorical structure analysis

1 Rumelhart (1975), Mandler and Johnson (1977), and Dressler (1978) explore the notion of text-oriented *grammars*. In his more recent work, however, Rumelhart has moved away from a grammar metaphor for text schemata towards a connectionist approach (see Rumelhart *et al.* 1986).

2 Meyer's system (e.g. Meyer 1985) is probably the closest to rhetorical structure analysis of the models mentioned above. Her work is also based on Grimes 1975.

3 Many of the assumptions of the model are based on Grimes 1975.

4 For most of the structures which contain an adjunct and a nucleus, either ordering of these elements is possible – that is, under certain conditions the adjunct can precede the nucleus, and under other conditions the nucleus can precede the adjunct. For some of the structures, however, different orderings are not possible; for example, it would be odd to find the evidence supporting a claim (adjunct) before the claim (nucleus). These asymmetries in ordering are not germane to the present study, however, and so play no role in the following discussions.

5 Embedding here is used to refer to text-structural embedding, not syntactic embedding.

6 I have taken the term *issue* from Reichman (1981), who uses it to refer to the main claim of an argument.

7 As with all instances of categorization, the prototype cases of each adjunct-type are clearly distinguishable from one another; in some cases, however, it is hard to make a convincing argument for an adjunct being one rather than another of these types. That is, it is often hard to say why something is being claimed to be an Elaboration adjunct rather than a Background adjunct. The lack of clear boundaries between these relations does not affect the basis of the claims about anaphora given in the next chapter, however, so I will not be overly concerned here with arguing for one interpretation or another. If there are defining criteria, they have not yet been fully established.

8 These adjuncts are probably better analyzed as members of a List structure – i.e., members of the same adjunct node – but in order to avoid confusion I have temporarily analyzed them as separate adjuncts.

9 The texts from which examples are drawn for this chapter are described in detail in section 5.2.1.

5 Anaphora in expository written English texts

1 For the anonymous articles in the newspapers and magazines, it is not possible to tell if the authors are native speakers of American English; nonetheless, the

articles are edited by native speakers of American English for an American English audience, so should be suitably native for the purposes of the present study. All the interactants in the conversations are identifiably native speakers of American English.

2 *A House of Lions* is unusual biography in that it does not attempt, as its main focus, to chronicle the linear passage of time in each biographee's life. In this regard, its psychoanalytic basis is crucial in making it an appropriate text for this study.

3 Texts that met these criteria were selected for inclusion in the study until what appeared to be a satisfactory representation of each source was achieved. The number of instances of each source is given below.

1 Twenty articles from the *Los Angeles Times*.
2 Twenty articles from *University Bulletin*.
3 Four chapters from *Bloomsbury: A House of Lions*, totalling approximately thirty pages.
4 Eleven articles from *People*.

A fairly even sampling of each source was thus obtained.

4 The texts ranged in length from two paragraphs to eight pages.

5 The terms *active* and *controlling* will be defined shortly.

6 See Ch. 3 for a thorough discussion of return pops and anaphora in the conversational texts.

7 But see the later discussion on internal articulation in general.

8 See Reichman 1981 for a discussion of return pops "reactivating" the items to which they return.

9 The pronominal reference to the nurse in the return pop follows the first pattern of pronominal return pops discussed above.

10 See section 5.6 for a discussion of non-structural factors in the choice of full NP over pronoun.

11 A related, but distinct, idea has been offered by Hinds (1979). Hinds suggests that paragraphs are organized into peak and non-peak sentences, where peak is correlated with informativity. Non-peak sentences are associated with pronouns, while peak sentences are associated with full NPs. One could see the unit-initial slot as high in informativity (most unexpected, least predictable content) and therefore a possible position for peak sentences.

12 Proposition 4 would probably have been done with a full NP in any case, because of the same-gender referent in the preceding adjunct. See section 5.5 for a discussion of same-gender referents.

13 It is clear that this formulation of the association between full NP and rhetorical structure could lead to circularity: the analyst could easily postulate that every time a full NP is encountered, a new rhetorical unit has been started. In future studies this circularity could be minimized by selecting several non-biased analysts familiar with the text-parsing technique to do the relevant analyses, or by first replacing all the appropriate NPs with blanks before doing the analysis. I feel that the association will stand, but it needs to be demonstrated in more rigorously non-circular ways before it can be counted as fully documented.

14 In some cases, strictly following one of the principles can make a genre-related statement, as in the obituary given below – an obituary of a young feminist, written by a feminist writer for a feminist audience:

> Joan Kelly, a leading feminist scholar, teacher, and activist, died of cancer on August 15, 1982, in New York City.
>
> A founding member of the Renaissance Society of America, *she* wrote an important book: *Leone Batista Alberti: Universal Man of the Renaissance*. Later, *she* was to question whether the Renaissance really did champion a universal humanist ethic for women as well as for men in her classic essay, "Did Women have a Renaissance?"
>
> *Her* early political activities marked the beginning of a lifelong commitment to combine activism with scholarship, practice with theory. She helped to found the United Federation of College Teachers and worked for a policy of open enrollment in the City College of New York as a practical means of overcoming discrimination against minority groups. During the 1960s she was also deeply involved in the antiwar movement.
>
> In the late 1960s *her* interests turned to feminism and socialism. . . .
> (*Ms*, December 1982)

The genre convention of beginning new rhetorical units with full NPs is ignored in this obituary, which almost certainly makes some statement about the relationship between the writer and the reader and the norms of the larger society.

15 Cf. Reichman 1981, in which it is claimed that only one referent is in high focus (and hence pronominalizable) at a time.

16 It is interesting to note in this regard that all the cases described here have involved the use of full NP where we could have expected pronouns; I found no non-structural factors which "induced" the use of pronoun where we could have expected full NP.

6 Anaphora in expository written and conversational English

1 I have avoided the term *spoken* in this study because it includes all texts produced by mouth – even orally produced monologues (such as classroom lectures or speeches). Since I have concentrated explicitly on non-monologic and spontaneous spoken language, I have preferred to use the narrower term *conversational*.

2 An excellent review of the literature on spoken and written language is provided in Akinnaso 1982. I have omitted discussion of much of that literature here, since it is not relevant to the phenomenon under study.

3 I see nothing wrong with defining these terms operationally, in terms of discourse structure, except that it further burdens already overworked terminology.

4 This measurement technique is based on the method developed in Givón 1983.

5 Cf. Wittgenstein(1958: 12):

> If you do not keep the multiplicity of language-games in view, you will

perhaps be inclined to ask questions like: "What is a question?" Is it the statement that I do not know such-and-such, or the statement that I wish the other person would tell me . . . ? Or is it the description of my mental state of uncertainty? – And is the cry "Help!" such a description?

6 It is possible that the recency model of anaphora was developed precisely because the focus of early work on anaphora was based on written, rather than conversational, English.

7 Obviously this statement should not be taken to indicate that participants immediately forget everything that was said in a closed environment – if something extremely hurtful was said, for example, the structure of the conversation will not automatically make the recipient of the wound forget the injury. What I mean is that this material is the least likely of any available to be brought up for future talk and thus it can be disattended to.

8 In Fox, forthcoming, b, I explore the possibility that a common algorithm could be developed for the basic anaphoric patterns of conversation and expository writing. The algorithm turns out to depend crucially on what is considered the main discourse unit of organization for each discourse-type, and this unit can only be specified by convention. So even the simplest pattern cannot be unified for the discourse-types examined.

9 I do not mean to claim here that this is the only possible reason for using a full NP when the referent is mentioned in the preceding clause. However, based on the non-quantitative work presented in Chs. 3 and 5, it seems safe to suggest that the demarcation of structural units is the major reason for this pattern.

10 I would not want to say that the second-pair part of an adjacency pair has an adjunct status with regard to the first-pair part: the two parts might have parity in the pair. We could thus say that an adjacency pair is equatable to a bi-nuclear R-structure.

11 For the purposes of this count, a reference was considered to be in a different-gender environment if the preceding clause contained (*a*) a subject NP that referred to a person of another gender, or (*b*) a mention of a referent of another gender, in any case role, if no other referent was also mentioned in the clause/proposition. That is, the italicized device in the first two of the hypothetical sentences below is considered to be in a different-gender environment, while the device in the last sentence is not considered to be in such an environment:

Susan was home with David, but *he* was unhappy
While Susan was in school, *Martin* was home with the kids
David was taking care of Susan, but *he* was unhappy

The method of counting thus possibly excludes some cases which are potentially relevant to the issue of "interfering" referents. Initial mentions of referents were excluded from this count, since their behavior is obviously not influenced by the appearance of other referents: they are always done with full NPs.

12 A reference was considered to be in the environment of "same gender" if a

referent of the same gender was mentioned in the preceding clause (*a*) as the grammatical subject of that clause, or (*b*) as the only referent in the clause. Initial mentions of referents were excluded from the count.

13 Recall that further description includes full NPs like *the lance corporal* which provide information that was previously unknown about a referent; classification includes full NPs like *the Swede* or *the child*, which provide no new information about the referent but only serve to place the referent in a category.

14 Phrases which convey negative or positive assessment are used with great elan – *the dirty bastard*, etc. – and are accounted for under Affect and Assessment.

7 Conclusions

1 Some of the points made in the following discussion have also been made in Fox, forthcoming, b.

2 The analogy with light as particle and light as wave is an apt one, since we can see light as both static and a dynamic process, depending on our purposes; see Young *et al.* 1970.

3 Except perhaps when viewed as a finished transcript by an analyst.

References

Akinnaso, N. 1982. On the differences between spoken and written language. *Language and Speech*, 25: 97–125.
Alvarado, S. 1986. OpEd: an editorial comprehension system. Talk given at University of Colorado, Boulder.
Atkinson, J, and Drew, P. 1979. *Order in court*. London: Macmillan.

Bates, E. and MacWhinney, B, forthcoming. Competition, variation and language learning. In B. MacWhinney (ed.), *Mechanisms of language acquisition*. Hillsdale, NJ: Erlbaum.
Biber, D. 1983. Towards a taxonomy of discourse types. MS.
Bolinger, D. 1976. Meaning and memory. *Forum Linguisticum*, *1*: 1–14.
– 1977. Pronouns and repeated nouns. Bloomington: Indiana University Linguistics Club.
Bosch, P. 1983. *Agreement and anaphora*. New York: Academic Press.
Bransford, J. 1979. *Human cognition: learning, understanding and remembering*. California: Wadsworth.
Britton, B. and Black, J. 1985. *Understanding expository text: a theoretical and practical handbook for analyzing explanatory text*. Hillsdale, NJ: Erlbaum.
Brooks, L. 1978. Nonanalytic concept formation and memory for instances. In E. Rosch and B. Lloyd (eds.), *Cognition and categorization*. Hillsdale, NJ: Erlbaum.
Brown, J. S. 1985. Cognitive and social ergonomics: from our house to Bauhaus. *Human–Computer Interaction*, *1*: 359–91.
Burton, D. 1980. *Dialogue and discourse*. London: Routledge & Kegan Paul.

Chafe, W. 1976. Givenness, contrastiveness, definiteness, subjects, topics and point of view. In C. Li (ed.), *Subject and topic*. New York: Academic Press.
– 1982. Integration and involvement in speaking, writing and oral literacy. In D. Tannen (ed.), *Spoken and written language*. NJ: Ablex.
Clancy, P. 1980. Referential choice in English and Japanese narrative discourse. In W. Chafe (ed.), *The pear stories: cognitive, cultural and linguistic aspects of narrative production*. NJ: Ablex.
Clark, H. and Haviland, S. 1977. Comprehension and the given–new contract. In R. Freedle (ed.), *Discourse comprehension and production*. NJ: Ablex.
Coulthard, M. and Montgomery, M. (eds.) 1981. *Studies in discourse analysis*. London: Routledge & Kegan Paul.

D'Angelo, F. 1975. *A conceptual theory of rhetoric*. Cambridge, Mass.: Winthrop.

de Beaugrande, R. 1980. *Text, discourse and process*. NJ: Ablex.

Decker, R. 1974. *Patterns of exposition* IV. Boston, Mass.: Little, Brown.

Dillon, G. 1981. *Constructing texts*. Bloomington: Indiana University Press.

Dressler, W. (ed.) 1978. *Current trends in textlinguistics*. New York: de Gruyter.

Du Bois, J. 1980. Beyond definiteness: the trace of identity in discourse. In W. Chafe (ed.), *The pear stories: cognitive, cultural and linguistic aspects of narrative production*. NJ: Ablex.

Duranti, A. 1984. The social meaning of subject pronouns in Italian conversation. *Text*, 4(4): 277–311.

Fillmore, C. 1968. The case for case. In E. Bach and J. Harms (eds.), *Universals in linguistic theory*. New York: Holt, Rinehart & Winston.

Fox, B. forthcoming, a. Anaphora in written popular narratives. In R. Tomlin (ed.), *Coherence and grounding in discourse*. Amsterdam: Benjamins.

– forthcoming, b. General principles and local patterns. *Text*.

– forthcoming, c. Morpho-syntactic markedness and discourse structure. *Journal of Pragmatics*.

Givón, T. (ed.) 1983. *Topic continuity in discourse*. Amsterdam: Benjamins.

Goodwin, C. 1981. *Conversational organization*. New York: Academic Press.

Graesser, A. and S. Goodman. 1985. Implicit knowledge, question answering, and the representation of expository text. In Britton and Black 1985.

Grimes, J. 1975. *The thread of discourse*. The Hague: Mouton.

Grosz, B. 1977. The representation and use of focus in dialogue understanding. Stanford Research Institute Technical Notes 5.

Guindon, R. 1986. Talk given at Symposium: Cognitive science: theory, methodology, and application to human–computer interaction. Boulder, Colorado.

Gundel, J. 1974. The role of topic and comment in linguistic theory. PhD dissertation, University of Texas, Austin.

Halliday, M. and Hasan, R. 1976. *Cohesion in English*. London: Longman.

Hinds, J. 1979. Organizational patterns in discourse. In T. Givón (ed.), *Syntax and semantics*, 12. New York: Academic Press.

Hinton, G. and Anderson, J. A. (eds.) 1981. *Parallel models of associative memory*. Hillsdale, NJ: Erlbaum.

Hirsch, E. 1967. *Validity in interpretation*. New Haven: Yale University Press.

Hopper, P. 1986. Emergent grammar and the a priori grammar postulate. MS.

– and Thompson, S. 1980. Transitivity in discourse and grammar. *Language, 56*: 251–99.

Iser, W. 1975. *The implied reader*. Baltimore: Johns Hopkins University Press.

Kamp, H. 1981. A theory of truth and semantic representation. In J. Groenendijk, Th. Janssen, and M. Stokhof (eds.), *Formal methods in the Study of language*, part I. Amsterdam: Mathematische Centrum.

Keenan, E. and Bennett, T. (eds.) 1977. *Discourse across time and space*. Southern California Occasional Papers in Linguistics 5. Los Angeles: University of Southern California.

Kintsch, W. 1974. *The representation of meaning in memory*. Hillsdale, NJ: Erlbaum.

Koffka, K. 1935. *Principles of gestalt psychology*. New York: Harcourt Brace.

Ladefoged, P. 1980. What are linguistic sounds made of? *Language*, *56*: 485–502.

Levinson, S. 1983. *Pragmatics*. Cambridge: Cambridge University Press.

Linde, C. 1979. Focus of attention and the choice of pronouns in discourse. In T. Givón (ed.), *Syntax and Semantics*, vol. 12. New York: Academic Press.

McClelland, J. and Rumelhart, D. 1985. Distributed memory and the representation of general and specific. *Journal of Experimental Psychology*, *114*: 159–88.

McHoul, A. 1982. *Telling how texts talk: essays on reading and ethnomethodology*. New York: Routledge & Kegan Paul.

McKeown, K. 1982. Generating natural language text in response to questions about database structure. PhD Dissertation, University of Pennsylvania.

Mandler, J. and Johnson, N. 1977. Remembrance of things parsed: story structure and recall. *Cognitive Psychology*, *9*: 111–51.

Mann, W., Matthiessen, C., and Thompson, S. 1982. Rhetorical structures report. MS.

Marslen-Wilson, W., Levy, E., and Tyler, L. 1982. Producing interpretable discourse. In Jarvella and Klein (eds.), Chichester: Wiley.

Matthiessen, C. and Thompson, S., forthcoming. "Subordination" and the structure of discourse. In J. Haiman and S. Thompson (eds.), *Clause combining in grammar and discourse*. Amsterdam: Benjamins.

Mayer, R. 1985. Structural analysis of science prose: can we increase problem-solving performance? In Britton and Black 1985.

Meyer, B. 1985. Prose analysis: purposes, procedures, and problems. In Britton and Black 1985.

– and Rice, G. E. 1982. The interaction of reader strategies and the organization of text. *Text*, *2(1)*: 155–92.

Ochs, E. 1979a. Transcription as theory. In E. Ochs and B. Schieffelin (eds.), *Developmental pragmatics*. New York: Academic Press.

– 1979b. Planned and unplanned discourse. In T. Givón (ed.), *Syntax and semantics*, vol. 12. New York: Academic Press.

O'Donnell, R. 1974. Syntactic differences between speech and writing. *American Speech*, *49*: 102–10.

Partee, B. 1984. Nominal and temporal anaphora. *Linguistics and Philosophy*, *7(3)*: 243–86.

Pomerantz, A. 1975. Second assessments. PhD Dissertation, University of California, Irvine.

Prince, E. 1981. Toward a taxonomy of given–new information. In P. Cole (ed.), *Radical pragmatics*. New York: Academic Press.

Reichman, R. 1981. Plain speaking: a theory and grammar of spontaneous discourse. Cambridge, Mass.: Bolt, Beranek and Newman, report 4681.

Reinhart, T. 1983. *Anaphora and semantic interpretation*. Chicago: University of Chicago Press.

Rubin, A. 1980. A theoretical taxonomy of the differences between oral and written language. In R. J. Spiro, B. C. Bruce and W. F. Brewer (eds.), *Theoretical issues in reading comprehension*. Hillsdale, NJ: Erlbaum.

Rumelhart, D. 1975. Notes on a schema for stories. In D. Bobrow and A. Collins (eds.), *Representation and understanding*. New York: Academic Press.

– , Smolensky, P., McClelland, J., and Hinton, G. 1986. PDP models of schemata and sequential thought processes. In J. McClelland and D. Rumelhart (eds.), *Parallel distributed processing: explorations in the microstructure of cognition*. Cambridge, Mass.: Bradford Books.

Sacks, H. 1971. Lecture notes. University of California, Irvine.

– , Schegloff, E., and Jefferson, G. 1974. A simplest systematics for the organization of turn-taking for conversation. *Language, 50*, 696–735.

Sanford, A. and Garrod, S. 1981. *Understanding written language*. Chichester: Wiley.

Schank, R. 1982. *Reading and understanding teaching from the perspective of artificial intelligence*. Hillsdale, NJ: Erlbaum.

Schegloff, E. 1979. The relevance of repair to syntax-for-conversation. In T. Givón (ed.), *Syntax and Semantics*, vol. 12. New York: Academic Press.

– 1981. Discourse as an interactional achievement. In D. Tannen (ed.), *Text and talk*. Georgetown, DC: Georgetown University Press.

– , Jefferson, G., and Sacks, H. 1977. The preference for self-correction in the organization of repair in conversation. *Language, 53*: 361–82.

Schenkein, J. 1978. *Studies in the organization of conversational interaction*. New York: Academic Press.

Serwatka, M. 1986. Untitled PhD Dissertation, University of Colorado, Boulder.

Sidner, C. 1983. Focusing in the comprehension of definite anaphora. In M. Brady and R. Berwick (eds.), *Computational models of discourse*. Cambridge, Mass.: MIT Press.

Tannen, D. (ed.) 1982. *Spoken and written language: exploring orality and literacy*. NJ: Ablex.

– (ed.) 1984. *Coherence in spoken and written discourse*. NJ: Ablex.

Terasaki, A. 1976. Pre-announcement sequences in conversation. Social Sciences Working Paper no. 99. University of California, Irvine.

Thavenius, C. 1983. *Referential pronouns in English conversation*. Lund Studies in English no. 64. Lund: Liberlaromedel Lund.

Tomlin, R., forthcoming. The syntax of reference in discourse production. In R. Tomlin (ed.), *Coherence and grounding in discourse*. Amsterdam: Benjamins.

Tyler, L. and Marslen-Wilson, W. 1982. The resolution of discourse anaphors: some on-line studies. *Text, 2(1)*: 263–91.

van Dijk, T. and Kintsch, W. 1983. *Strategies of discourse comprehension*. New York: Academic Press.

Voloshinov, V. 1973. *Marxism and the philosophy of language*, tr. L. Matejka and I. R. Titunik. New York: Seminar Press.

Webber, B. 1983. So what can we talk about now? In M. Brady and R. Berwick (eds.), *Computational models of discourse*. Cambridge, Mass.: MIT Press.

Winterowd, W. (ed.) 1975. *Contemporary rhetoric: a conceptual background with readings*. New York: Harcourt Brace Jovanovich.

Wittgenstein, L. 1958. *Philosophical investigations*. New York: Macmillan.

Young, R., Becker, A., and Pike, K. 1970. *Rhetoric: discovery and change*. New York: Harcourt, Brace, & World.

Author index

Subject index

text-types: 1, 138–40
  comparability of: 138–9
  see also genre
texturing: 77
topic: 139–141
topic continuity: 56, 118; *see also*
  anaphora, traditional theories of
transcripts (of conversations): 6
  transcription notation: 6–8

turn-taking: *see* conversational analysis

use (accomplishes context): 16–17, 40, 93,
  97–8, 104, 112

validity (of analysis): 91–2

writing process: 93–4, 112, 144, 150
  stability of product: 142–3